SMOKER'S Art

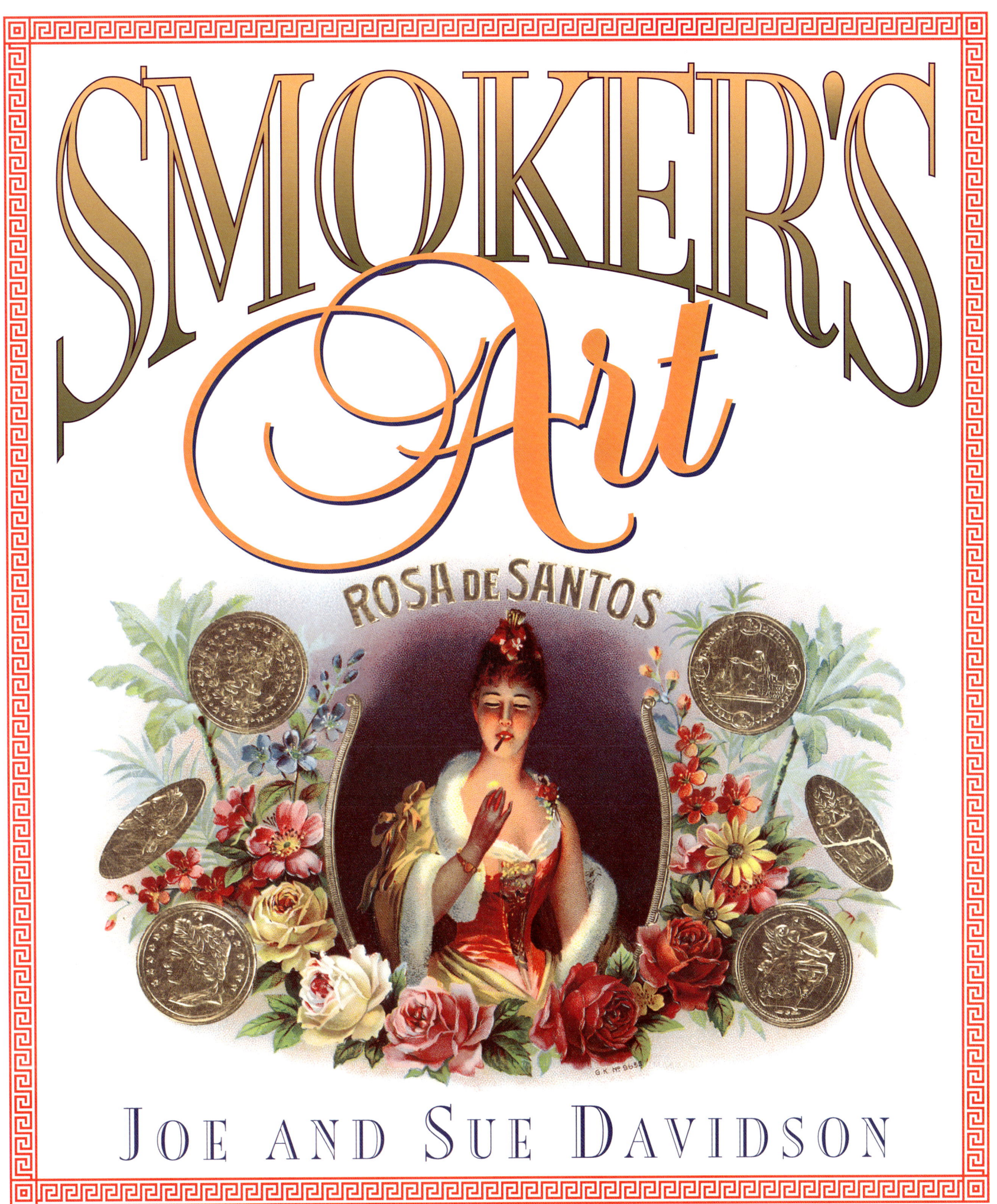

JOE AND SUE DAVIDSON

WELLFLEET

Copyright © 1997 The Wellfleet Press

A Division of Book Sales, Inc.

276 5th Avenue, Suite 206

New York City 10001

All rights reserved.

No part of this book may be reproduced or transmitted in any form

or by any means, electronic, or mechanical, including photocopying,

recording, or by any information storage and retrieval system,

without permission in writing from the publisher.

Publishing Director: Frank Oppel

Interior Design: The Great American Art Company

ISBN 0-7858-0866-3

Manufactured in China

Contents

Preface 4
Acknowledgements 6

1. **SMOKING & SMOKERS**
   Historical Perspectives 10

2. **LITHOGRAPHY**
   Printing Processes 12
   Lithographers 16

3. **COLLECTING**
   The Art of the Collector 22
   Values & Rarity 24

4. **TOBACCO ART**
   Original Art 28
   Progressive Proof Books 30
   Proofs 34
   Sample Labels 40
   Variations 52

5. **CLASSIC BRANDS**
   American Classics 58
   American Brands with an International Flavor 74
   International Classics 84
   Cuban Gold 104

6. **CLASSIC THEMES**
   Famous Men 116
   Famous Women 134
   Sports & Recreation 148
   Animals 158

7. **THE PACKAGING ART**
   Textuals 170
   Trimmings 178
   Cigar Boxes 208
   Cigar Bands 216
   Caddy Label Art 228
   Cigarette Pack Art 242

Resource Information 248
The Authors 250
Index 251
Picture Credits 254

Preface

Nearly a decade has passed since the first copies of *The Art of the Cigar Label* began to appear in major book stores throughout the world, and what a decade it has been! The die-hard base of fewer than 1,000 tobacco ephemera collectors in the 1980s has since multiplied at least twentyfold — due in part, we hope, to the publication of that book, now in its fourth printing.

The Art of the Cigar Label filled a necessary void, and fed the fledgling collector's thirst for knowledge, but it was also the result of a series of events that created an interest in tobacco, its history, and the art that helped to market it.

By 1989, cigar labels had been elevated from flea-market status to exhibition in some of the most prestigious department stores and fine art galleries. Upscale mail-order houses, including Nieman-Marcus and Levengers, sent out millions of color catalogs offering beautifully framed original cigar label art as gifts and decor, introducing them to an entirely new audience.

The cigar smoking craze, which has produced over eight million new cigar smokers in the United States since 1992, has further increased tobacco art awareness, with the birth of thousands of new cigar stores, cigar bars, cigar-friendly restaurants, and over a dozen specialty cigar and pipe magazines, both national and regional.

Unwittingly, the anti-tobacco movement has contributed dramatically to public awareness in more than one sense. Its campaigning further reinforces in many people's minds that tobacco has been, and still is, an important part of American history that may soon disappear as we once knew it.

Adding to the public's awareness is the Cuban National Heritage Foundation's traveling display of Cuban-American history that is now appearing in many major museums and historical societies across our country, featuring — what else? — cigar label art!

Although a few pragmatically challenged doomers-and-gloomers have labeled this new appreciation and awareness of both tobacco advertising art and stone lithography as a mere fad, we truly believe that the die is now cast, and this unique and spectacular art form is finally receiving its well-deserved recognition in the art world. (Interestingly, the number one collectible in the United States from 1890 to 1915 was also tobacco-related, namely, cigar bands!)

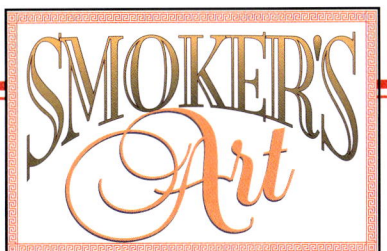

What is most important about cigar labels — besides the fact that they are outstanding works of art and early lithography offering a unique insight into American history — is that they exist in a truly limited number compared to other collectibles. The best estimate given today by those who rescued them from dusty old warehouses and abandoned cigar factories is two to three million. This total includes not only those images that were found in bundles of 500, but also the extremely rare lithographer's proofs. This is quite sobering when you consider the army of potential collectors coming on stream, but more importantly, it is almost minuscule when compared to the billions of what are now called "contrived collectibles," such as baseball cards, phone cards, action figures, and limited editions.

Some may consider *Smoker's Art* to be a sequel to *The Art of the Cigar Label*, but it is much, much more. True, we will bring you up to date on the events that have transpired over the past decade, including new discoveries of labels and historically important information. More importantly however, we will attempt to give you a broad overview of the many uses of the lost art of stone lithography in promoting tobacco products during the "Golden Age." While showing you hundreds of new images, we will also try to provide insight into establishing rarity, assessing value ranges, identifying stone lithography, and the history behind it all. Although we have created a specific section dealing with trimmings — the art that appears on the outside of the box — we have in many other sections included both exterior and interior art. This was done for reasons of design and layout as well as image availability.

While we have relied heavily on our own research for this book, many of the most interesting and enlightening facts have come to us from dedicated collectors, who dug through old tobacco journals and tracked down a few surviving lithographers and cigar makers.

This work has been a labor of love for both of us, and we are sure you realize that the greatest gift we can share with you is knowledge. Having said that, we also realize that many specifics cannot be covered in minute detail in a single work such as this. But rest assured, you do have additional recourse. For any questions concerning your specific interests, contact The American Antique Graphics Society, P.O. Box 924, Medina, OH 44258.

Acknowledgements

Our never-ending search for knowledge and information relating to the fascinating world of *Smoker's Art* has been a labor of love for us for over two decades. During the creation of *The Art of the Cigar Label* in the 1980s, we were blessed to have found a small but dedicated group of historians, librarians, museum curators, retired lithographers, cigar rollers, and early collectors who ferreted out many previously unknown facts that we enjoyed sharing with you. Now, thanks to the steady growth of new collectors, we have inherited a virtual army of researchers and detectives, bursting with the energy and the desire to glean more and more information in an effort to add more pieces to the puzzle.

As in any emerging collectible field, you will always find a few opportunists and plagiarists seeking to capitalize on the efforts of others, but the vast majority of newcomers to this field truly love the art and history associated with it and work tirelessly, searching for any possible leads that will help satisfy their craving for new discoveries. Their excitement is contagious, and they are proving daily that there are still more treasures to be discovered by those willing to work at it.

Although we still relied on many of the "old timers" for their help in this book, we are still in awe of the time and energy spent by some of the newest collectors who pursued a variety of avenues we had never dreamed of. Brent McQueen, a young executive and newlywed, found time in his hectic schedule to track down the heirs to the Heppenheimer and O. L. Schwencke Litho companies. His efforts paid off, with boxes of spectacular labels and priceless information delivered to his doorstep. Gerry Schmidt, a former San Francisco crime scene detective, now uses his talents to track down cigar industry history — and, of course, some great labels for his own collection. (When we said we had inherited an army of researchers and detectives, it was more than a metaphor. Collector Si Bass is a retired U.S. Army major, and Aaron Hemphill, who has been a multi-faceted collector all his life, is a former Air Force Captain.)

If we had the time and space to list the résumés of all our contributors, it would probably raise more questions than answers as to why such talented people chose to pursue this hobby over others. In many cases, we are amazed that these individuals have any free time at all. (Then again, remember the old saying, "If you want

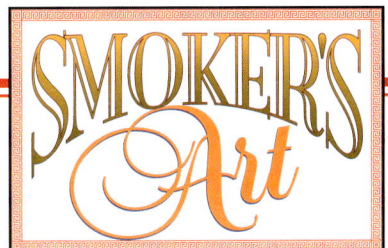

to get something done, ask a busy person to do it.") Selfishly, we hope that many of them will opt for early retirement so they can spend even more time playing detective.

The number one label scout in Eastern Pennsylvania has to be Jerry Striker, who also holds down a full-time, high-pressure job in the graphic arts field. The local paper dealers in his area are praying that Jerry doesn't take early retirement, since he already beats them to the punch with great regularity.

Another graphic arts pro who has never failed us is Stewart Graham from Northern Ohio University. Stewart is past president of the prestigious International Printing House Craftsmen and always has his antenna up for anything related to graphic arts history.

Some of the part-time historians and label detectives who have dedicated their energies to the hunt include Ken and Ginny Nichols, Sid and Selma Emerson, David Beach, Kevin Karr, Ruth Giordano, Cathy Peru, Steve Gilbert, Mark Eatough, Darren Hirsch, Jake Rosenfield, Lon Schwartz, Aaron Sigmond, Larry Morone, John McCarthy, Bernie Schonfeld, Chuck Cordero, Rick and Betty Hall, Dan Double, Tony and Deanna Broadbent, Kelly Schultz, Ed and Laura Harrison, and Giacinta Bradley Koontz, Director of the Harriet Quimby Research Conference.

As pleased as we are with the army of new collectors who have shared their discoveries with us, we are doubly pleased that the main core of old-timers who have worked with us through the years also took time to contribute to this effort. (We hope you realize that the term "old timers" refers more to their years in this field than their chronological age.)

Topping our list this time around is Ray Kane, past president of Consolidated Litho. Not only has he selflessly made himself available for all our questions on numerous occasions, he probably holds the record for donations of labels, samples, and proof books to museums, historical societies, and universities. We like to think of him as the Andrew Carnegie of the graphic arts world.

Another classy New Yorker, still going strong at the age of 88, is our friend George Schlegel III. When he merged Schlegel Litho with Snyder & Black in 1969, he had the foresight to rescue all the old cigar labels,

caddy labels, posters, and master reference books. Even more valuable than these artworks is his crystal-clear memory of Schlegel history, which he has been kind enough to share with us over the years.

Another family historian whose friendship we treasure is Tampa historian Thomas Vance. His great-grandfather was Ignacio Haya, founder of the Sanchez & Haya Factory no. 1 in Tampa, Florida. When historians and academics in Tampa need answers to perplexing questions, they usually have to rely on Tom. Tom lived it; they write about it. Once known as Tampa's best-kept secret, he is now getting the recognition he deserves. Rarely is a display on Tampa or cigar industry history unveiled without the curators asking Tom to critique it ahead of time to avoid embarrassment.

What Tom Vance is to Tampa history, Tony Hyman is to the world of cigar boxes. Although Tony is best known for his syndicated radio show and books on collectibles, his primary interest is, and always has been, cigar boxes. Without Tony, there would not be a section devoted to cigar boxes in this book.

Our discussion of cigar bands has been enriched by the knowledge and experience of two of the most dedicated band collectors in the world, Joe Hruby and Louis Vandeuren. Joe and Louis have enjoyed their hobby for over 100 years collectively and have watched it stumble and then grow to new heights with the recent emergence of hundreds of new collectors.

Another multi-talented individual and antique graphics lover who has always been there when we needed him is John Grossman, founder and president of the Gifted Line in Port Richmond, California. A world-renowned artist and author, John fell in love with Victorian graphics early in his career and now utilizes images from his own extensive archives on a variety of products, from calendars and greeting cards to wrapping papers and gift boxes. John's collection has grown to the extent that he now has a full-time curator, Dave Mihaly, on his staff.

As Dave will tell you, a curator couldn't possibly handle these outstanding artworks, created for the tobacco industry, without falling in love with them. If you don't believe Dave, just ask David Wright, curator of the U.S. Tobacco Museum or Helena Wright, from the Smithsonian.

We can't forget Mark Trout, who calls from all parts of the country with research questions and answers. We are all lucky he had the foresight to see the beauty in labels.

Although their collections aren't as big as the Smithsonian's, the museum-quality art and historical artifacts in the collections of the following individuals are no less important: Mike Stinnett, Aaron Davidson, David and Larry Lisot, Jay Last, Louis Galetta, Leif Erickson, Judy Hill, Jake Gilbert, Leonard Lasko, Howard Rierson, Don Pickett, Bob Kane, Ron Scheiber, Bob Spirtas, Teresa Masten, Van Hart, Alberto Bustamante, and Susan and Marty Weiner.

1. Smokers & Smoking Historical Perspectives

Historians agree that tobacco played a major role in every step of America's development. Tobacco originated in America, it was the nation's very first business, and it was American ingenuity that brought it to its present level of sophistication. The history of tobacco is the history of America itself. Although the first recorded documentation of this "holy herb" was written by Romano Pano — a Spanish monk who accompanied Christopher Columbus on his second voyage to America — anthropologists and sociologists suspect that tobacco has been used by American Indians for over 2,000 years.

Many history books credit the Spanish with introducing tobacco on a commercial basis in 1556; however, the Portuguese were cultivating it in Brazil as early as 1534. By 1548, over a dozen Portuguese settlements were exporting tobacco to Lisbon. Jean Nicot, the French ambassador to Portugal, introduced tobacco to France in the 1560s, and it is from his name that the word *nicotine* is derived.

Tobacco's potential as a consumer product was quickly recognized by the trade-conscious Dutch. Since Holland was a Spanish possession during the mid-16th century, the Dutch had early access to this bewitching plant, and Dutch consumption of tobacco outstripped that of much larger countries such as England and Germany. By the late 1500s, sailors around the globe were smoking and chewing this virtuous vegetable, but it was Sir Walter Raleigh who moved it quite a few steps up the social ladder by introducing pipe smoking to the English court.

In spite of its ever-increasing popularity around the globe, tobacco certainly had its share of early detractors, and a variety of severe punishments were stipulated in law for its use. England's King James I passed laws establishing mutilation as punishment for taking a pinch of snuff and hanging on the gibbet for smoking a pipe, while monarchs from Russia, Turkey, Persia, and India imposed the death penalty for smoking.

Notwithstanding such severe penalties, smoking proliferated in these countries and, like true politicians, monarchs soon realized that this custom could provide a source of additional tax revenues.

In the colonies of Virginia, tobacco was as good as gold. Colonial governors accepted their tax payments

in tobacco leaf, and the clergy went to court when the government tried to pay them with money! (For decades, clergymen were paid 16,000 pounds of tobacco per year as their salaries, and the ups and downs of the market made tobacco much more attractive to them than money.)

Tobacco also played a major role in financing our Revolutionary War. Robert Morris, a Philadelphia businessman — whose image appears on a cigar label titled *Financier* — negotiated the sale of enormous amounts of tobacco to France for money and war materials. In appealing to the American public to support his troops, George Washington stated, "If you can't send money, send tobacco."

Prior to the Civil War, the majority of tobacco consumers in the United States used snuff or chewing tobacco, or smoked a pipe. During press coverage of the Civil War, early photos, daguerreotypes, and engravings of many of the heroes and generals depict them smoking cigars, including the ultimate cigar smoker of the time, Ulysses S. Grant.

By 1870, cigar consumption reached the one-billion mark in a population of only 40 million, and by 1920 reached an all-time high of 8.2 billion. Interestingly, that was also the year in which the use of cigarettes surpassed that of cigars. While cigarettes still maintain their lead, the dramatic resurgence in the popularity of cigars may soon change that ratio.

No one can predict what lies in store for the tobacco industry, but undoubtedly it has weathered much more severe attacks by purists and special-interest groups. Proving that history does repeat itself, here are just a few of the laws concerning tobacco written by the Puritans.

- No one under the age of 20 shall take tobacco without a certificate from a physician.
- Citizens may smoke only after dinner (no mention of sex), and no more than two people can smoke in the same house at the same time.
- Tobacco cannot be taken in public except on journeys of ten miles or more.
- In many parts of New England, a fine was imposed for smoking outdoors. (Interestingly, some of the proceeds from the levied fines were awarded to the informants. What a neat way to subsidize your income and punish your enemies at the same time. Josef Stalin must have studied early American History.)

Tobacco is a dirty weed — I like it.
It satisfies no normal need — I like it.
It makes you thin, it makes you lean,
It takes the hair right off your bean,
It's the worst darn stuff I've ever seen — I like it!
"Tobacco" by Graham Lee Hemminger.

2. Lithography Printing Processes

In the hope of giving a helping hand to those interested in building a collection of high-quality artwork — whether created for the tobacco industry or any other purpose — we will try here to give you enough facts to let you distinguish stone lithography [Greek. *lithos* stone; *graphos* write] from photomechanical printing, and to recognize some of the in-between processes. (It would be impossible to cover *all* the graphic processes used. In any case, many of the intaglio, relief, and planographic processes were seldom used for label art.)

The art of stone lithography was born out of poverty and necessity, when Aloys Senefelder of Prague found himself, at the age of 23, forced to provide for a family of nine. A playwright, Senefelder was also a true inventor — never cowed by negativism, always hopeful, ingenious, and tireless. When he found it too expensive to have his plays published, he decided to find an inexpensive way to become his own publisher and printer.

His first breakthrough came in 1796, when he found that the local Bavarian limestone made an excellent printing surface for a crude relief process. It was soft enough to be grooved with a tool to make a raised image for printing, yet hard enough for repeated impressions.

In 1798, he gave to the world a third printing process, neither relief, as from type, nor intaglio, as from etching. It was a flat surface (planographic) method that opened whole new horizons. Senefelder discovered that if an image is drawn directly on the flat stone surface with a wax crayon, the wax penetrates the porous stone and becomes fixed. The stone, now ready to print on, is dampened with water, the moisture being repelled by the areas containing wax, but absorbed by the other areas. When an ink roller is passed over the surface, no ink is taken up by the damp areas, but the lines and dots of the wax drawing attract the ink and hold it until transferring the clear ink image to the paper passing through the press. Senefelder called his

process "chemical printing" — we know it today as stone lithography. It proved to be a fast, inexpensive method that produced a true image which, with all its tonal effects, rivaled the velvety qualities of mezzotint.

1.

Although the above description deals with single-color lithography, practically all of it is applicable in describing the process of multi-color printing, or chromolithography.

In 1808, Senefelder published a book with illustrations by Albrecht Dürer. The quality of the illustrations revealed the possibilities of stone lithography as an art medium as well as for commercial printing. Lithography is truly art for the artist, who is totally involved from beginning to end — preparing the stone, drawing the image, selecting the ink colors, and supervising the printing.

Frederick Goulding, a celebrated printer of both etchings and lithographs, said it well: "Lithography is not a reproduction; it is a replica, a multiplication of copies; not a facsimile or a paraphrase, but the actual drawing. That is where it differs from so many other processes."

Benjamin West, an American artist working in England, created one of the first works of true artistic merit on stone, "An Angel at the Tomb of Christ," which received worldwide acclaim.

But it was in France, starting around 1809, that lithography found its heart and soul, blossoming with the works of such renowned artists as Honoré Daumier, Théodore Géricault, Eugène Delacroix, and Francisco Goya. The lithographs of these artists command top dollar today.

In 1836, also in France, Godefroi Engelmann and his son Jean invented a method of color printing which came to be called chromolithography. Using red, yellow, and blue pigments, the Engelmanns and painter William Wyld together produced a seven-stone color image from crayon and lithographic inks. This was indeed a major step forward, only one generation since Senefelder's first efforts, and a giant advance beyond hand-colored lithographs.

Stone lithography in the United States reached its peak with the

2.

work of Louis Prang, who came to Boston from Germany. Prang developed methods using up to 25 stones to achieve unusual color layering, adding an embossing process for the creation of imitation brush strokes and a superb lacquering process for the finished product. Given the title "Father of Chromolithography" in the United States, Prang was responsible also for the introduction of the first American greeting cards in 1837.

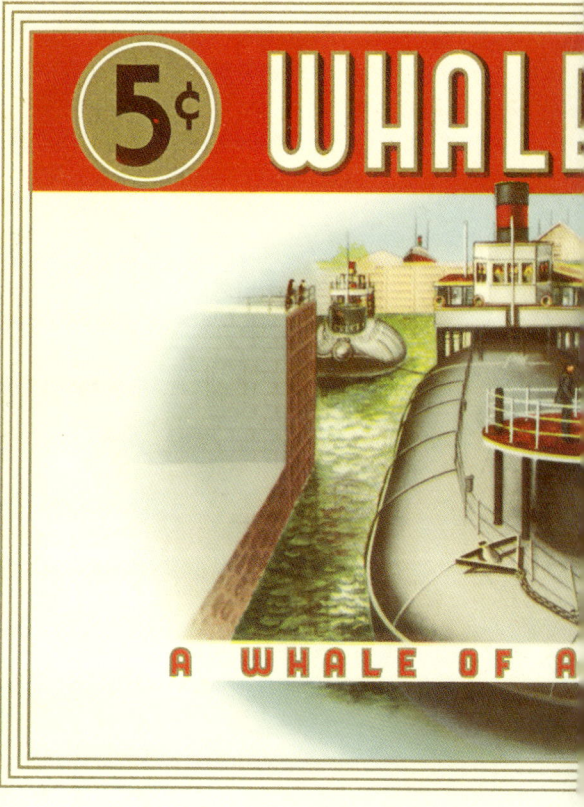

3.

The earliest chromolithographs were made up of areas of solid color printed beside each other. What Prang developed was a technique that simulated the entire color spectrum by intermingling small color areas, which, after the 12 (or 20 if necessary) separate impressions had been made, resulted in the complete range of hues and tints necessary for a realistic final image.

By the turn of the century, the process had become even more sophisticated through the use of hand stippling. In simple terms, stippling is the use of a series of intermingled dots that produce varying degrees of shading. This process had been used in engravings as far back as the 16th century, and was brought into prominence by the artist Bartolozzi in the late 18th century. This concept of color rendition allowed the printer to produce an extremely accurate reproduction of the artist's original painting.

As lithographers worked diligently to continuously upgrade the quality of their product, they also sought a way to speed up production in an effort to meet the demand for a greater quantity of high-quality advertising artwork.

In order to eliminate some of the time-consuming labor of hand stippling, Benjamin Day, an eastern lithographer, invented a "screen" process whereby large areas could be quickly and effectively filled with dots. The screen — a gelatin-like material embossed with small raised dots — was lightly waxed and then pressed onto the desired area of the stone, leaving that area with thousands of waxy dot impressions ready to accept ink. Obviously, some hand stippling was necessary to blend image transitions, but thousands of tedious hours were saved by the use of this new method.

Another problem was the stones. They were very heavy and hard to handle (many weighing as much as 600 pounds), and they broke easily. When it was found that zinc or aluminum surfaces could be prepared so that they produced prints with all the characteristics of those from stones, thin plates of these metals were substituted. Thin versions of such metal plates, which could be curved and attached to a cylindrical roller, were used to adapt the method to the new rotary printing press, which allowed greater speed and efficiency. This

printing method, along with the stone lithography that was still used by many printers, made up the lion's share of the color printing methods used until the late 1920s, when the photomechanical process gained in popularity.

The photomechanical process, which is still in use today, is a technique whereby the original artwork is photographed through a set of color filters, separating the various colors of the image into three individual colors: yellow, red, and blue. A fourth color, black, is also created to simulate realistic shading and contrast. These four negatives are combined with screens containing arrays of closely spaced dots, and each is placed over a separate photosensitive metal plate. (The screens have been rotated to different angles for each of the colors so that the arrays of dot patterns interfere with one another as little as possible.) Each plate is exposed to light, resulting in four printing plates containing information (dots) for each color. When the image is printed using these plates, each set of dots prints in its own ink color, in some cases overprinting other colors, and these combinations simulate all color shades and hues. The dots can be made so marvelously fine that there can be up to 400 per linear inch. For ordinary printing purposes, a screen having 120 dots per inch is generally used; coarser newspaper photos use 60 dots per inch.

Sadly, this new four-color process eliminated the need for the lithographic artist. Plates could now be produced photographically straight from the original art. Of course, this greatly reduced the printing cost, but it also brought to an end to the era that gave us some of the finest examples of chromolithography ever produced.

To help you identify the methods of printing we have discussed, following are some examples of the crayon method of chromolithography, the stipple method, and the photomechanical process.

Crayon Lithography
1.   *Little Bo-Peep.*   A typical 1870s style.

Stipple Art
2.   *First National.*   Over and above the millions of hand-applied dots, imagine how long it took to draw all these bricks!

Photomechanical
3   *Whale-Back.*   Some excellent examples of early offset printing. Note the photo rosettes.

Lithographers

Since a detailed account of turn-of-the-century lithographers would probably require over 300 pages and 50,000 words, we will attempt to concentrate on those firms that had the strongest ties and made significant contributions to both the tobacco industry's efforts and the advancement of the art of stone lithography. As the beneficiaries of their efforts, we, as collectors, should treasure any and all of the art and information that has survived over the last century.

The nucleus of today's collectible base came from the bundles of labels that were discovered in the 1970s as abandoned cigar and plug tobacco factories were dismantled. The icing on the cake in this burgeoning collecting field was the discovery of what many call the "super-rare" images recovered from the files and archives of a few lithographic giants. The very fact that anything survived at all borders on the miraculous, since there are many horror stories of entire archives being taken to the dump or incinerator.

When Central Litho (formerly Johns and Otis) moved during the Depression in 1932, they sent truckloads of labels and posters to the dump, since they didn't have space at their new location. Morgan Litho, another major lithographer in Cleveland, burned thousands of circus and magic posters that would now be worth a fortune.

Controversial baseball team owner and successful entrepreneur Marge Schott of Cincinnati is the daughter of a cigar box manufacturer. When many cigar makers opted to use the cheaper cardboard box over the handcrafted wood boxes that her father produced, he became so disgusted that he began burning all his label stock in the furnace. Young Margie thought they were so beautiful that she began rescuing piles of labels to keep as mementos, and was ridiculed for her efforts. Nevertheless, Marge prevailed. Not only does she still have a spectacular label collection, she also has the last laugh!

The most critical period for the survival or destruction of such rare treasures was usually during the sale or merger of the litho firm. Obviously, it took a special breed of individual or individuals to make the decision to save these ephemeral objects, sometimes at great expense, when the easy way out was to dump everything.

One example is the acquisition of 400-year-old Klingenberg Brothers Litho by the Gundlach Group, a

1. Advertising poster for Calvert Litho.

large conglomerate owned by doctors Bernhard and Bina von Schubert. Since the Gundlach Group was already involved in a variety of graphic-related projects, ranging from advertising and publishing to calendars and executive gifts, Gebrüder Klingenberg was a logical acquisition. The bonus from this acquisition for Bernhard and Bina was the spectacular archive of labels, stones, and proof books that had survived two wars, including thirty-eight days of saturation bombing by the British. Miraculously, most of the archive's treasures were intact, and the von Schuberts have incurred tremendous costs in time and money to preserve them for future generations.

George Schlegel III also deserves an accolade as a bona fide rescuer. When he merged Schlegel Litho with Snyder & Black in 1963, George arranged to have all the file cabinets — filled with old labels, proofs, and correspondence — taken to the basement of his home, where he enjoyed them for many years before finally selling them to a few dedicated collectors in the 1980s. A product of the U.S. Naval Academy and Princeton University, George started working for the prestigious family firm in 1932 and assumed the presidency in 1946.

2. Bernhard von Schubert with progressive display in his conference room at Klingenberg Litho.

George kept Schlegel Litho in the limelight during his tenure as president through his activities with a variety of organizations, including the Young Presidents Organization, The Metropolitan Lithographers Association, The Young Lithographers Association and the Lithographic Technical Foundation, now known as the Graphic Arts Technical Foundation. In spite of his great accomplishments, George will undoubtedly be best remembered for saving the Schlegel Archives.

Another notable rescuer with ink in his veins is Raymond P. Kane. His 50-year career in the printing business started in 1939 with the U.S. Printing and Litho Company. Interestingly, U.S. Printing & Litho once owned American Litho, a major producer of labels and fine art prints, but sold it to Consolidated Litho in 1932 before Ray joined the company. In 1958, U.S. Printing & Litho merged with Diamond-Gardner to form the well-known Diamond National Corp. As executive vice-president, Ray was instrumental in its expansion to well over 100 plants and 17,000 employees.

Although he missed acquiring the American Litho archives in the 1930s, fate would not be denied, and in 1972 Ray bought Consolidated Litho, including its archives, which contained works by American Litho and many of its predecessors. While one of Ray's talents included an ability to "turn companies around" — buying failing companies and making them profitable — he admits that his love and respect for the antique graphics held by Consolidated strongly influenced his decision to buy them out.

3. George Schlegel III.

4. Raymond P. Kane.

After bringing Consolidated to new levels of strength and profitability, Ray decided to donate a large portion of its archives to a number of universities and historical societies where, he thought, they would be appreciated and displayed. Unfortunately, that was not always the case. However, as an old-time art dealer once said, "A curator's mismanagement is a collector's windfall." So, on a brighter side, many of these important pieces of historical graphics will eventually end up in deserving hands!

Ray deserves an accolade for rescuing these important artworks, as many of his contributions did find a home in reputable institutions, where thousands of art lovers can enjoy them for generations.

There are many other positive stories about such amazing rescue missions, including Calvert Litho, AutoKraft Box Co., and others, but these few examples show how the efforts of a few can benefit so many.

Calvert Litho is another name that will live on in graphic arts history, not only for its work for the tobacco industry, but also for its dedication to quality workmanship. Its permanent motto was "The Model Shop," indicating its mission to set exemplary standards of excellence for the industry. As one can tell from its advertising poster claiming "We make perfect labels," Calvert was quite proud of its reputation. And while some may interpret this claim as boastful, there is an old saying: "If it's the truth, it's not bragging."

Calvert produced some of the most beautiful high-quality artwork for a variety of products, but their cigar and caddy labels are especially prized, since so few have survived. Interestingly, Calvert in many cases designed original artwork for some cigar companies, but it soon lost the accounts due to its refusal to match the competition's lower prices.

Brands you may remember, such as *Dante, Tungsten,* and *Iroquois* were lost to Schlegel Litho, while brands you may identify with Consolidated Litho — *Lyra, Dime Bank,* and *O'San* — were initially produced by Calvert. Discovering any of these images that denote Calvert Litho on them is a rare find indeed.

The marriage between the tobacco industry and the pioneering lithographers that worked so closely with them was obviously made in heaven. And as the popularity of tobacco use — especially in the form of cigars — grew, so did the commercial competition.

The need for new, beautiful, and more exciting labels motivated cigar makers to offer outrageous sums of money to lithographers who could produce the most spectacular artwork. Instead of spending the resulting bonanza on personal creature comforts, these early, mostly Germanic artisans plowed it all back into their graphic arts businesses, investing in state-of-the-art technology. A list of these firms would include names such as Witsch & Schmitt, Heppenheimer & Maurer, L. E. Neuman, Schumacher & Ettlinger, Schmidt Litho, Harris, O. L. Schwencke (later Moehle, then American Colortype), Krueger & Braun, and Steiner.

These pioneers established the benchmarks for all future lithographers, and although their buildings have crumbled and their presses have been sold for scrap, their legacy remains with us in the beautiful labels that have survived.

5. Thomas Calvert with his staff artists, ca. 1890.

Lithographers of Note

Ackert Company, Cincinnati
American Colortype, New York & Chicago
American Label Company, New York
American Litho, New York
Baltimore Litho, Baltimore
Bartholemew Litho, Scotland
G. M. Boyd & Company, New York
Calvert Litho, Detroit
Central Litho, Chicago
Central Litho, Cleveland
Chicago Box Company, Chicago
Cole Litho, Chicago
Conover Engraving & Printing, Coldwater, MI
Consolidated Litho, New York
Cosack & Company, Buffalo
Courier Litho, Buffalo
H. H. Doehler & Company, New York
Donaldson Bros., New York
Wm. M. Donaldson Company, Cincinnati
Eastern Colortype, New York
Eckstein & Hoffman Litho, New York
Isaac Friedenwald Litho, Baltimore
J. Guenther & Company, St. Louis
Guenther & Mueller, St. Louis
George S. Harris, Philadelphia
George S. Harris & Son, New York
George S. Harris & Sons, Philadelphia, New York & Chicago
Gerhard & Heymanns, Germany
Hatch Litho Company, New York
Thomas H. Heffron, New York
Heffron & Phelps, New York
A. C. Henschel Company, Chicago
C. B. Henschel Company, Milwaukee
Heppenheimer & Maurer, New York
F. Heppenheimer Sons, New York & Chicago
Heywood, Strasser & Voigt, New York
A. Hoen & Company, Richmond, VA
H. Hoklas & Sons, Peoria, IL
F. M. Howell Company, Elmira, NY
Johns & Company, Cleveland
Kaufman-Pasbach-Voice, New York
J. H. Keithly, Cincinnati
Ketterlinus, Philadelphia
Klingenberg Litho, Germany
Knight & Company, Cincinnati
Koelle-Mueller Label Company, St. Louis
Kreft Label & Printing, St. Louis
Krueger & Braun, New York
Lancaster Litho, Lancaster, PA
Geo. F. Lashler, Philadelphia
Maryland Litho, Baltimore
Mensing & Stecher, Rochester
Michigan Litho, Grand Rapids
Moehle Litho, New York & Chicago
Möller, Kökeritz & Co., New York
T. A. Myers & Company, York, PA
Louis E. Neuman & Company, New York
New York Label Publishing Company, New York
Otis Litho, Cleveland
Pasbach-Voice, New York
Petre, Schmidt & Bergman, New York
A. Ward Phelps, New York
Progress Litho, Cincinnati
Sackett & Wilhelms Litho Company, New York
Geo. Schlegel Litho, New York
Schlegel Litho, New York
Schmidt & Company, New York & Chicago
Schmitt & Company, New York
Hermann Schött, Germany
Schumacher & Ettlinger, New York & Chicago
O. L. Schwencke, Brooklyn, NY
Schwencke & Pfitzmayer, New York
Seifert & Schneffel, Milwaukee
Sheip & Vandergrift, Philadelphia
W. A. Shine, San Francisco
Shober & Carqueville, Chicago
Stahl & Jaeger, New York
Stecher Litho Company, New York
E. Steffens Litho, New York
William Steiner & Sons, New York
Louis C. Wagner, New York
Albert Weise, Philadelphia
Western Label Company, Milwaukee
Western Label and Supply, Leavenworth, KS
Wiegand & Frank, Germany
Witsch & Schmitt, New York
Charles A. Wulff, New York

3. Collecting
The Art of the Collector

True collectors are a special breed, regardless of their specialty or passion. It is a documented fact that collecting at an early age is one of the four signs of giftedness in a child. When you look at the credentials of some of the best-known collectors in history, you will probably agree. Over and above any intellectual superiority, true collectors possess an unmeasurable quality that every employer and athletic coach yearns to find in new recruits. Not only is that quality unmeasurable through any academic testing or sophisticated electronic devices, many people have a problem describing it in words. While such adjectives as "zealous," "fervid," "passionate," and "go-getter" come close, we like old-timer Sid Emerson's colloquialism, "fire in the belly." Some of the better-known possessors of this quality — which carried over into their collecting habits — include Julius Caesar, Thomas Jefferson, J. P. Morgan, William Randolph Hearst, and Malcolm Forbes Sr. Notwithstanding the impressive collections held by the British Museum, the Vatican, the Hermitage, the Louvre, and the Smithsonian, it is estimated that over 50% of the most important art and artifacts in the world exist in private collections. The museums have the money, but true collectors have the fire in the belly!

It is a documented fact that collections of art and artifacts have always held top status as spoils of war. From ancient times through to World War II, conquerors traditionally established special teams of historians and experts whose sole purpose was to follow the troops into a conquered city to "liberate" all the treasures they could find. By the end of World War II, the Germans had amassed such an enormous quantity of art and collectibles that they began storing some of it in old salt mines and caves. Taking a page out of history, the American forces sent teams of experts, along with convoys of trucks, to "liberate" these treasures from eastern Germany before the Russians took over. Unfortunately, some of our historians and experts were motivated by personal greed and destroyed priceless artifacts, such as swords and crucifixes, by popping out the jewels and melting the gold.

Some other casualties of that war included millions of dollars' worth of rare books and prints, which were

destroyed when German cities were "saturation" bombed by the U.S. and British Air Forces. During our visit to the Klingenberg archives in Germany in 1988, we were gratified to discover that they had stored a modest number of spectacularly gilded cigar labels in a sub-basement that miraculously survived the bombing — which gave us a whole new level of appreciation for any Klingenberg image we may own. Whether they are from Germany, Cuba, or even the good old U.S.A., we should all be thankful that any of these artworks, which at one time were considered ephemeral, have survived.

In our never-ending quest to discover more and more of these "survivors," we are constantly asked, "How can I build a valuable collection?" First of all, don't use intrinsic value as your main criterion. When you build a great collection, the intrinsic value will probably surpass any IRA or mutual fund you might gamble on. Compare the individual who builds a collection as a labor of love and is shocked, but pleased, to discover it is worth over $100,000 to the investors who bought truckloads of baseball cards in the 1980s and are still staring at them today. Not only did these "investors" miss the enjoyment of building a viable and valuable collection, they missed the whole point completely. We have yet to interview an old-time cigar band collector whose original goal was to make money. Fortunately, many meticulously cared-for collections are now paying tremendous dividends to those willing to part with them.

So how do you build a viable collection? Buy what you like. Trust your instincts, your eye for good artwork, and your ability to investigate the history of both the artwork and the subject portrayed in it. When buying an item, as in any business transaction, ask the seller to supply you in writing with any background information about it — this should play a role in your decision as well as the item's authenticity and future value. The collecting world is permeated with self-appointed gurus who need to bolster their own self-esteem or who just like to hear themselves talk, and this is one way to shorten the dialog. Another point to remember with these "experts," is to ask them where they got their information. "Some guy told me" may be good enough for them, but it's an insult to your intelligence.

We did discover one catalog that stated: "We guarantee all items in this catalog to be genuine, but if you should discover it to be a reproduction, we will refund your money." Wow, what nice guys! They have the use of your money, while you run around the country trying to have the item authenticated. Thanks, but no thanks.

Once you have confidence in a dealer and in your own abilities, try to avoid focusing on any of the "trendy" areas, such as Indians, sports, Blacks, etc. It's always great to add these pieces to your collection, but it is much wiser to build a collection with an eclectic mix of subject matter, which will probably pay off in the long run. As your collection grows, it can evolve from categories to sub-categories, but for a great, well-rounded collection, try to include a progressive, some proofs, a few samples (along with examples of all the trimmings), and an actual box.

Values and Rarity

Assigning values in any field of collectibles is an inexact science at best. Auctions give us one barometer, but the size and makeup of the audience, along with the auction's timing and degree of promotion can sometimes result in unrealistic high or low prices that may never be repeated. One thing is certain: prices have climbed steadily since we produced *The Art of the Cigar Label* in 1989. But that is a natural phenomenon, considering the increased awareness of tobacco and its history caused by the dramatic growth in cigar smoking and anti-smoking publicity.

Have cigar label prices really climbed that dramatically? Evidently not, compared to other categories in the antique graphics world. For example, in 1989, a set of royal octavo Audubon birds sold for $8900. In 1996, three sets that surfaced fetched from $27,000 to $52,000, the prices being determined primarily by the condition of the prints. In that same year, you could have purchased an 1862 *Johnson's Atlas* with hand-colored maps for $75 to $125. Today, map dealers are excited when they find one for under $1500!

While there is a degree of inflation involved in any evaluation formula, it is basically a matter of supply and demand — for a product that exists in a relatively low, finite quantity. This factor is determined by history.

With regard to cigar label art, as the collector base continues to grow, remember that over 95% of all images discovered exist in quantities of under 5,000. Going a few steps further, the best estimates and research show that over 70% exist in quantities of under 2,000, and more than half of all the images available exist in quantities of under 100!

With over eight million new cigar smokers coming on stream since 1993 — and an unlimited number of potential collectors — how long would it take for many of these images to disappear from the market? If you applied the same formula (relating rarity to price) that exists in the coin world, a large number of labels would probably be selling for over $25,000!

Although we should be pleased that cigar labels first appeared in flea markets — where we gobbled up many bargains ourselves — the very structure and marketing practices of the individuals involved unquestionably caused more harm than good. For example, Dealer X stumbles across a find of only 100 labels in a warehouse or garage sale in Pennsylvania. Lacking faith in the either the product, his flea market customers, or even his own abilities, he quickly sells 80 of them to four other dealers, who now have twenty each for sale. Instantly,

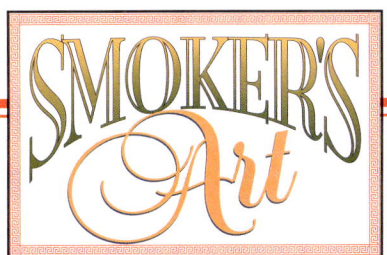

you have five different dealers offering the same image at the same time, causing any potential buyer to surmise that there must be a ton of them out there! Scary as it may sound, this scenario has happened on more occasions than anyone might imagine, stigmatizing many great images and completely confusing new collectors.

"Common" is a poorly chosen term used by many to describe labels. We like John Grossman's term, "multiples," which implies there is more than one copy of any given image, but does not imply that the image is undesirable. Remember, one man's trash is another's treasure! When someone says "that's common" to us, we always ask how many examples they have. Actually, we're not being unkind, since it usually makes a person stop and think about what is and isn't common. Remember, if you divide 1,000 labels by 50 states, that comes to only 20 per state — and less again, when you consider the international market. Only the forces of supply and demand and a long waiting period will correct such "common" viewpoints, but by that time, the damage will have been done.

Another area that has caused even more confusion and controversy has been the adoption of a grading system for labels similar to that used in the coin and baseball card world. Experts agree that this one area has caused more problems and created more opportunities for scoundrels than any other in the coin and baseball card world.

In the antique graphics world, a short but concise description is usually given identifying specific areas of aging or damage. For example, a buyer may have no problem with a half-inch tear on the edge of a graphic piece, but does not want any foxing (brown age spots). Conversely, another collector might tolerate a few glue spots but definitely doesn't want any creases.

A typical description found in print catalogs reads: "Good condition, 1″ tear (not near image), some foxing on edges." Now the buyer knows exactly what he or she is getting and will probably buy it, or at least know what questions to ask. (Interestingly, the term "good condition" in the coin world is often applied to a coin so worn you can hardly see the date. In in the flea market world, it might describe a label that has probably been on the bottom of a birdcage for at least a month!)

One collector — fed up with the ambiguity of the terms used by dealers — has sent us his own analysis of their rating system: "*mint* = acceptable to a cataract patient; *excellent* = looks good from 12 feet away;

very good = has only one hole, one tear, one fold, one large stain, and was soaked out of a book with dirty water; *good* = multiply 'very good' by ten." Dealers who have adopted this descriptive system, whether through laziness or intent to deceive, are learning that many new collectors are too sophisticated to fall for it.

Throughout this book, we have assigned value ranges to artwork using the asterisk system that was so well-received in *The Art of the Cigar Label.* Instead of a maximum of four asterisks however, we have added a fifth, which can be interpreted in a number of ways, from "off the chart" to "good luck finding one!" Obviously, this maximum will not be assigned to many images, but it does give you an insight into what some people call "super-rare"!

VALUE RANGES

These categories have basically been assigned by the marketplace. Of course, subject matter, quality, desirability, and, to a lesser degree, quantity affect the category assignment. With the dramatic growth in the number of new collectors, we can safely predict that many of the images seen in this book will "move up" a category or two!

★ UNDER $25

★★ UNDER $75

★★★ UNDER $150

★★★★ UNDER $500

★★★★★ CONSIDERABLY MORE

With regard to rarity, we do know in some cases how many copies of a specific image were found after interviewing the individuals who actually cleaned out many of the old cigar and box factories. Although this gives us an initial benchmark, we must try to clarify the difference between the number of images discovered and the number that survived in saleable condition. Considering the fact that in most cases, the images may have been sitting in one location for over 50 years, chances are that extreme heat, water damage, and a variety of rodents and insects have reduced their number by at least 20%.

Even if an unopened bundle of 500 labels appears to be reasonably clean and undamaged on the outside, it is likely that at least 10% are foxed with brown spots (usually the top and bottom ones), and another 5% are either out of registration or have smudges.

In over twenty years, we have yet to see the perfect bundle! For example, approximately 100 bundles of large 6 X 9 *American Citizen* labels were found in a barn in Quaker City, Ohio. One hundred bundles times 500 equals 50,000 labels, right? Think again. This barn had more openings in its walls than a corn crib, and the soot from a wood stove that covered everything (including the labels) was half an inch thick. The fact that we were able to rescue 20,000 labels for use in the first edition of *The Art of the Cigar Label* was an absolute miracle. Of the 30,000 remaining, over 20,000 were beyond saving and had to be destroyed. (Too bad the VG-G rating system wasn't in effect back then — we probably could have sold them!)

So what is the final outcome of this 50,000-label discovery? Well, 20,000 are out of circulation — sitting on bookshelves throughout the world — over 20,000 went up in smoke, and the rest were wholesaled to a variety of dealers. It appears that, just as coin dealers had to in 1980 (after millions of silver coins were melted), we need to ask the operative question, "How many have survived?"

A few other titles were found in large quantities and are no longer available in quantity at any level. You may recognize the following names: *Round-Up*, the majority of which was sold to Japan; *Mark Twain*, most of which were framed and used as executive gifts; and *Covered Wagon*, which disappeared virtually overnight. History shows that 10,000 examples of anything, including limited editions, can disappear very quickly in a country of over 250 million people!

Most importantly, buy what you like, not what you think will go up in value.

Time, inflation, and a growing base of collectors affect values in almost all collectible fields. Since you are collecting items that can never be reproduced, and only finite numbers exist, label collecting appears to be a lot more attractive than investing in the stock market!

4. Tobacco Art Original Art

Sharing the spotlight with progressive proof books for the "one of a kind" category is the original art produced by lithographers' staff artists. Whether it was a portrait for a vanity label, an image stolen from an old master, or something from the artist's imagination, an original piece of art and a keyline drawing were needed by the stipple artist before he could put the first dot on any lithographic stones with his wax crayon.

Much rarer than progressives, the few pieces of original art for tobacco labels that have been found were usually discovered in old file cabinets and had never been transferred to stone. If you happen to have a piece of original art, chances are that, except in a very few instances, you are unlikely to find a matching label.

After interviewing a number of old-time lithographers, we discovered that in most cases, after the image was transferred to stone, they saw no need to keep the original art and it was destroyed.

Since very few pieces of original art for tobacco products have ever reached the block in any major auction house, we still don't have a fair benchmark for assigning realistic values. However, if the values realized by original art in other areas of collecting, such as book covers and magazines, are any barometer, you could be talking about some serious money!

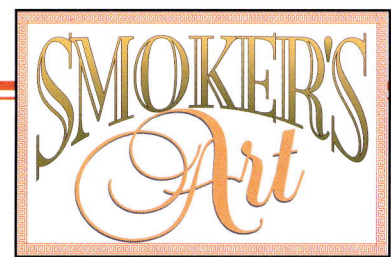

This example of original artwork was created in March, 1879 by Carl Mummert, a renowned painter and illustrator, and a member of the Düsseldorf Academy. Produced for Gerhard Heymanns Litho, Mulfort, Rheydt, Germany.

Progressive Proof Books

Just as one picture is worth a thousand words, one progressive proof book is worth more than a thousand words when one is trying to explain or understand the concept of stone lithography. Whenever we are asked to provide a display of antique graphics for a university or library, we always bring along an actual litho stone and a progressive proof book for people to examine. Once they see the number of stones required, the need for perfect registration, and the intense labor involved in the entire process, they have much more respect for the stone litho images on display.

We believe that every antique graphics collector should own at least one progressive proof book, although we are reasonably sure that in the near future there won't be enough to go around.

Sticking to our philosophy that people should buy what they like, many of the same parameters used in buying labels or prints apply to the purchase of a progressive proof book: subject matter, number and brightness of colors, and condition, condition, condition!

Unfortunately, many progressive proof books received a tremendous amount of wear and tear, since they were referred to quite frequently by the job foreman or workers with dirty hands. Adding to those problems, over half of all books that have survived were disassembled a number of times to replace a page after a new stone was changed or added. "Corrected Stone," written in pencil by the job foreman, is one of the most common notations you will find on new pages.

Progressive proof books also come in a variety of formats, depending on the lithographer. European progressive proof books (which are the hardest to find) display the finished image on the last page in the book, as opposed to U.S. lithographers, who placed the finished image first.

Whether because of individual idiosyncrasies or possibly expediency, American progressive proof books also differ dramatically in the number of impressions or pages. In their early years, the progressive proof books used by the American Litho Co. contained a true "progression" of the colors — red; yellow; red and yellow combined; blue; red, yellow, and blue combined — leading up to the finished image.

Some lithographers included not only an impression of each color, with its appropriate ink, but also an impression using black ink, in order to check patterns not easily seen with the lighter-colored inks.

Less than 10% of all progressive proof books discovered to date will include a "keyline" drawing — similar to paint-by-number kits — used by lithographers to double-check the blending of colors.

One other feature used by some, but not all lithographers was the addition of a "color bar" somewhere on each page. Not only did this show each color ink that was used, but in many instances, the stock number of the ink was included to make the lithographer's job easier.

No matter which format you end up owning, the most important factor is that you have the finished image and one page for each color that was used.

With regard to values, much more data is available since our study in 1988, following almost a decade of auction results and details of prices realized at these auctions. Although a few damaged, incomplete, or minimum color books have sold for less than $100 (usually $85 to $90), the lion's share of merely average subjects still command $500 to $1500, with some reaching the $2400 level.

We would all love to find the "informationally challenged" museum or historical society curator who doesn't like or understand stone lithography and take a collection off their hands for pennies on the dollar, but it appears that those days are just about over.

In the world of collectibles, a "one-of-a-kind" is always the most valuable and coveted piece a collector could own, and in the world of stone lithography, that's a progressive proof book!

TOBACCO ART • *Progressive Proof Books*

John Drew was an early stage actor. This eleven-color progressive for a nail tag gives you an idea of how each color was separated from the original art. The final proof also features a color bar for each ink used.

Progressives of trimmings are becoming quite popular for framing because of their size.

P ress proofs have always been an integral part of the graphic arts world and are still used today. Excluding the time needed to produce and submit an original pencil sketch, which was then followed by a finished piece of water-color art, the lithographic artist spent a minimum of two months in completing all the stones needed to produce a label. Records from Calvert Litho show they took up to four months. By comparison, today's printers can produce a four-color set of film positives in less than four hours.

During the stone litho era, lithographers could assume, but never know exactly what the finished product would look like until that very first proof came off the press. Once they had that first proof in their hands, they could then make any minor (hopefully) changes in the stipple dots on one or two stones, or strengthen or soften some of the ink colors. If you are fortunate enough to own examples of both the proof and the finished label, you will probably be able to spot a few subtle, and in some cases, dramatic differences.

For neophytes who have never seen or handled an original proof, the most obvious differences between it and the finished label are: (1) a proof is usually not embossed, and (2) a proof has visible registration marks — lines and crosses placed at key points to insure proper alignment of the stones.

One other feature usually reserved for proofs was a series of color bars which showed each color ink in its pure state. Not every lithographer included color bars, but for those that did, it was a quick reference guide, since each ink color variation had a number assigned to it.

Although it is generally assumed that lithographers usually pulled up to six proofs, that number could possibly be greater. But rest assured, these proofs would have noticeable variations.

In our personal experience of owning, examining, and appraising hundreds of proofs, along with the fact that we were the very first to examine the Schlegel and Calvert Litho archives, we have never seen more than three proofs of any one label. But whether one or even ten examples of a proof exist, they obviously rank extremely high on the rarity scale, surpassed only by a piece of original art or a progressive proof book.

With regard to values, prices realized at auctions since 1989 have ranged from $35 to $1550. Since "averaging" such extremes is not realistic, the true middle-range price for a proof today appears to be $125 to $250.

Remington ***** American Litho rendition of Remington artwork probably produced after his death.

TOBACCO ART • *Proofs*

1. *Champion* **** Although this Appleton, Minnesota brand featured a knight in armor, the artist included a vignette of a farmer plowing his field to attract his rural Minnesota customers. Produced by Schmidt Litho.
2. *Chimo* **** This unusual and unique solid red background surrounding a jolly monk smoking was produced by Geo. Schlegel Litho.
3. *Crack Shot* **** American Litho produced this image during the career of Annie Oakley, but they probably didn't want to pay a royalty.
4. *Ivory King* ***** The F. H. Berning Company of Cincinnati featured an Indian elephant on this brand. Produced by Calvert Litho.
5. *Liberty Hall* **** Geo S. Harris and Sons Litho chose the signing of the Declaration of Independence for this label.
6. *Mataafa* **** Calvert Litho produced this label for the Duluth Cigar Co. to commemorate the sinking of the steamer Mataafa during the great storm of November 28, 1905, in which nine lives were lost. Although we have seen many examples of acts of heroism celebrated on a cigar label, this is the first we have ever seen commemorating a disaster.
7. *Middy* **** The Great Lakes Cigar Co. in Detroit, Michigan commissioned Calvert Litho to produce this pretty young sailor girl for their nautical customers. As you can see from the registration marks by the title, Calvert used the same stone to produce the outer label.
8. *Paul Revere* **** Calvert Litho produced the famous ride of Paul Revere for – who else? – The Revere Cigar Co.

1.

4.

2.

9. *Phantoma* **** Spectacular artwork by Heywood, Strasser and Voigt Litho featuring an old-timer reminiscing about the good old days while enjoying his cigar.
10. *Press Agent* **** This image is a Calvert Litho artist's conception of a flashy press agent. Interestingly, he has an Elks pin in his lapel.
11. *Sagamore* ***** The Iroquois Cigar Company of Flint, Michigan chose the image of the famous chief, Sagamore, for one of their brands. Produced by Calvert Litho.
12. *Sassy Sue* **** Victorian girl flanked by ornate art nouveau decor. Schlegel Litho.
13. *Swastika* ***** Long before Adolf Hitler's Nazi party adopted this symbol, American Litho produced this image relating the long history of the swastika. This brand survived for over 30 years.
14. *Untitled, Frog Man* ***** An imaginative concept produced by Klingenberg artists over 50 years before the movie *The Creature from the Black Lagoon*.
15. *Untitled, Girls smoking* **** A superb example of what can be accomplished by a talented lithographer with only a few colors. Produced by Klingenberg Litho.

Sample Labels

Sample labels were not exactly an instant hit when cigar label collecting began to catch on in the 1970s. Like proofs, they were "different" from the standard fare of images rescued from the old cigar factories, and the writing at the bottom seemed to detract somehow from their overall appeal. By the 1980s, a few astute collectors began to realize that these labels, since they were only samples, might never have been actually selected by a cigar maker to go into production. Hence, there was a possibility they could be unique. The answer to that possibility is both yes and no. Yes, large percentages of images produced as samples were never chosen, and those that survived did so only in sample form. The "no" part of the answer is that lithographers mailed out thousands of small booklets to each and every cigar maker or box maker they could find.

But where are these samples now? No one knows for sure, but logic dictates that they were probably treated like today's junk mail, and if the cigar maker saw nothing of interest, sadly enough, he filed it in the wastebasket. This theory is further reinforced by the fact that there are no great "hoards" of samples out there waiting to be purchased.

Whether it is commodities or collectibles, supply and demand will always the rule the marketplace.

Regardless of whether the collection you are building is specialized by subject matter or lithographer, or just generally eclectic, we truly believe that you should include at least a few samples, since they are an important part of the overall picture.

If you do own one or more sample labels, odds are that they were printed by an American lithographer and probably came out of a sample book.

In a very few instances, some lithographers mailed out loose labels upon special request, but in most cases labels were stapled together inside an attractive cover that promoted the firm. These "booklets" usually contained from 6 to 12 images.

Some of the other forms of sample books that have been discovered include the road salesman's sample book, which usually contained 80 to 100 images.

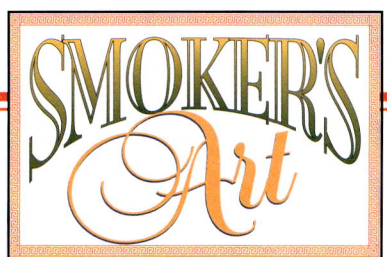

The granddaddy of all true sample books has to be the showroom sample book, which contained anywhere from 500 to 800 images and featured an ornately embossed cover.

Equally as large, but not nearly as fancy, were the sample books kept by cigar box makers and the master reference book, kept in the shop area by the printing foreman. These large books contained examples of every label that they had on stone — it was obviously much easier to use them for reference than to run over to the stone room and examine stones. Labels taken out of such books, easily identified by the cursive notes written on them, should properly be classified as "examples" instead of samples.

In the fine art world, where rare manuscripts and natural history prints often originated as book pages, it is a fact that many old books are now more valuable intact than broken up into separate prints. If this analogy holds true, it might be wise — for reasons of historical value and rarity — to keep intact any sample books you might discover.

Hero's Welcome **Klingenberg Brothers maintained the German policy of stapling labels together with a descriptive sheet giving their name and address, despite the fact they maintained a New York sales office. This image was also produced with the title, *Heroica.***

1. *Call Again* ** A commonly used title in the cigar world, both textually and pictorially. This simple but unique textual design was created by Hubley Printing in York, Pennsylvania. Notice their claim: "Cheapest Labels in the Market"!
2. *Crack Team* ***** The Louis E. Neuman lithographers created some unique and beautiful non-embossed crayon images in their early work. By the time embossing and gilding had arrived, they got even better.
3. *Dick Deadeye* *** Heppenheimer & Maurer's artists tried to appeal to the nautical crowd with this one-eyed gunner's mate who supposedly never missed.
4. *Domestic* *** G. M. Boyd was probably trying to create a label for locally grown tobacco, since the lady doesn't appear to be a housewife or servant.
5. *El Padre* ** This image did make it to a cigar box, but we don't know how long the paternalistic brand lasted. Produced by Heffron & Phelps.
6. *Fancy Stock* *** Harris Litho artists tried to hopefully associate expensive livestock with this brand of cigars.

4.

FROM
G. M. BOYD,
Successor to Boyd & Co.

No. 1014. **Domestic**, Ins., fancy, $25.00 per 1000 $2.65 per 100.
No. 1015.   "   Outs.,   "   12.50 per 1000 1.35 per 100.
ALSO BLANK.

6.

GEO. S. HARRIS & SONS,
CIGAR BOX LABELS AND TRIMMINGS,
718-724 Arch Street, Philadelphia.
BRANCH HOUSES: S. E. Corner Grand and Bowery, NEW YORK.
No. 53 State Street, CHICAGO.

No. 2935 $20.00 per 1000 $2.10 per 100
ALSO FURNISHED BLANK

7. *Friendly Tip* *** Horse racing was a popular theme for cigar art, and this one, by Wm. Steiner & Sons, has only positive connotations.
8. *Good Record* *** Trotting horse race. O L. Schwenke's artists loved to feature action scenes on many of their labels, and this is an excellent example of their talents.
9. *Good Record* *** Compared to O. L. Schwenke's version of *Good Record,* this Lancaster Litho example appears rather unimaginative and generic.
10. *Immatchable* *** Although the label shows that Louis Wagner & Co. was based in E. 20th Street in New York, their printing plant was in Germany.
11. *La Amadora de Habana* ** Generally known for their creativity and imaginative label art, Witsch & Schmitt evidently tried to copy their German competitors, who almost always tried to incorporate cupids into the over all image.

7.

8.

9.

10.

IMMATCHABLE

No. 8209 — INSIDE — $2.40 NET PER 100 — ALSO
No. 8211 — OUTSIDE — 1.20 — BLANK

Louis C. Wagner Co., 43 East 20th Street, N. Y.

RECORD

Also Blanks.

Per 100 Net

171 RANDOLPH ST.
CHICAGO, ILL.

11.

LA AMADORA DE HABANA
TABACOS SUPERIORES

WITSCH & SCHMITT,
94 Bowery, New York.

No. 1541 FLAP, No. 1543 TAG.
ALSO BLANK.

RECORD.

ANA

ANK.

Lancaster Lithographing Company.
OFFICE AND SALESROOMS:
34-36 East Chestnut Street, - LANCASTER, PA.
IN 1,000 LOTS.

12. *Little Joe* ** F. M. Howell, a cut-rate label discounter who targeted the small "mom & pop" cigar maker, showed in this example how a cigar maker could have any photo placed in one of Howell's blank stock labels. Remember, F. M. Howell was not a lithographer, but a printer and box maker.
13. *Maru* ** Hermann Schött Litho. Many German lithographers opted to mail individual samples to their U.S. accounts in a format in which all the pieces in the set were stapled together, with a sheet of paper providing the printer's name and address instead of the labels themselves.
14. *Mogul* ** Removed from a Calvert Litho master reference book, this image for the *Mogul* brand appeared on a variety of products other than cigars, including canned pineapple and other food products. Note the cursive notation "Lagora Fee & Co." March 31, 1909.
15. *Old Nut* *** The artists at Schumacher & Ettlinger evidently felt that a sizable number of people could identify with this title which they produced in 1883.
16. *Old Rose* ** A. C. Henschel was basically a label broker and used a number of lithographers to produce their labels. They had their very best labels printed in Germany, and even used F. M. Howell in Elmira, N.Y. for their "low end", as this appears to be.

13.

12.

14.

15.

No. 6306. Inside. | No. 6307. Outside.
$25.00 per 1000. | $15.00 per 1000.

ALSO BLANK.

SCHUMACHER & ETTLINGER,

32, 34 & 36 Bleecker Street, New York. | 89 Randolph Street, Chicago.

A. C. HENSCHEL & CO.
310 - 312 W. SUPERIOR ST.
CHICAGO, ILL.

No. 7812 Ins
No. 7813 Outs $1.75 per 100

16.

17. *Optic* **** Unique art by Johns Litho, featuring an eyeball staring at you, possibly hoping to hynotize the potential buyer.
18. *Papa's Own* *** "The Light of the Home." Otis Litho was obviously referring to both the child and the cigars.
19. *Rose Bud* ** Moehle Litho, the successor to O. L. Schwenke, started incorporating the band associated with the main subject in many of their samples. Although this sample was probably much earlier, many collectors believe that this is a portrayal of Marion Davies, "Rosebud" in the famous Orson Welles movie, *Citizen Kane*.
20. *Smiles* ** This image, which was directed toward the French-Canadian smoker, features a girl in period costume with her French poodle. Wm. Beck was a label broker. The image was actually produced by L. E. Neuman of New York.
21. *Swallow Tail* ** Early Krueger & Braun image of a barn swallow carrying a rose. Notice the four vignettes on the sides are not complete.

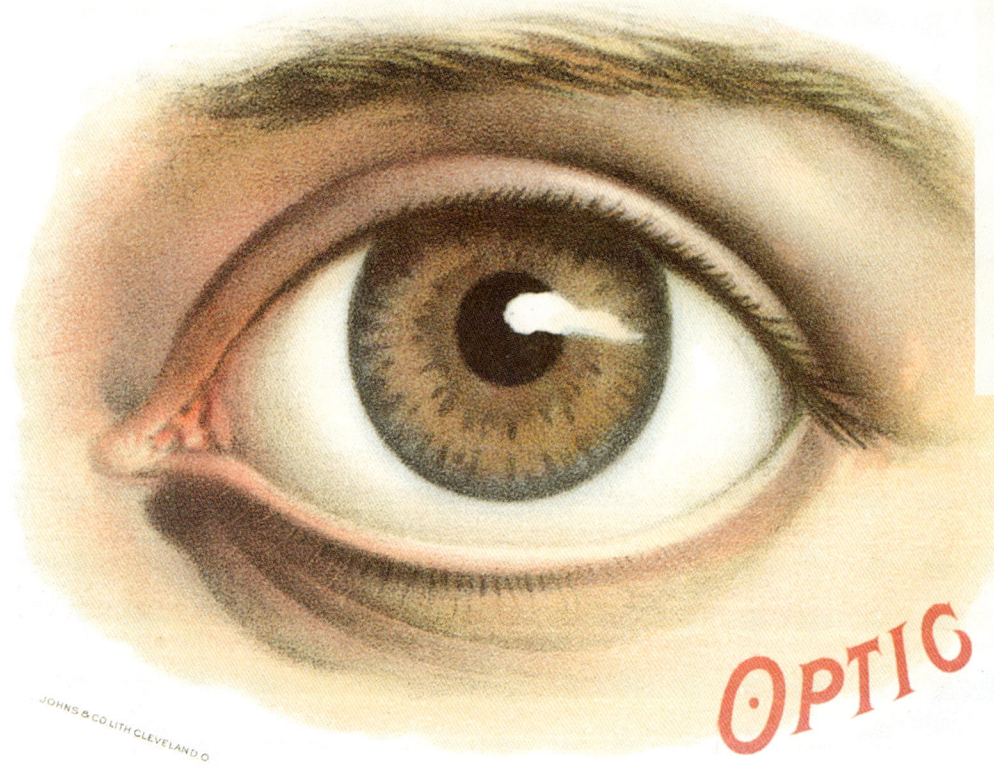

19.

ROSE BUD

THE MOEHLE LITHOGRAPHIC CO.
CLARENDON ROAD & E. 37TH ST. BROOKLYN, N.Y.
BRANCH OFFICE: 171 E. RANDOLPH ST. CHICAGO, ILL.

NO. 576 INS $1.80 PER 100
NO. 577 OUTS   .90 " "   (ALSO BLANK
NO. 578 TAG   .50 " "
NO. 579 BAND   1.00 PER 1000)

ROSE BUD

21.

SWALLOW-TAIL

NO. 305 INS.   ALSO BLANK $25.00 PER. 1000
 " 306 OUTS.   "   " $15.00   "   "
KRUEGER & BRAUN. 59 & 61 GOERCK ST. NEW YORK

22. *The Test Cigars* ** Mensa, the high-I.Q. society, hadn't come into existence when this image was produced in 1899, but it appears that "tests" were popular at the time. It does appear that Schmidt & Co. was trying to show just how ornate a textual label could be. They also note on the edge that they will custom print and emboss any name, or this image could be purchased blank, and the customer could letterpress a name as needed.

23. *Winsome Ways* ** Not only was Geo. Schlegel Litho known for their great artwork, they also provided the largest percentage of romantic themes compared to their competitors. This sample is dated 1896.

25. *Untitled, Hand holding cigar & match* ** American Litho learned quickly that the cigar maker may like the image but not the title. Instead of making changes in the stones, they could quickly add by letterpress any name, in any color. This label has a 1904 copyright date.

26. *Untitled, Ocean liner* **** This Stecher Litho sample incorporated a subtle number five on the boat's sail, implying that the cigars still cost five cents.

27. *O. L. Schwenke sample book.* This is the typical salesman's sample book, which usually held 80 to 200 different images.

28. *Louis E. Neuman, George Schlegel, Möller, Kökeritz & Co. sample books.* Three examples of direct-mail sample books, which were sent out by the thousands to old and new customers alike, announcing the newest and latest images. Interestingly, Möller, Kökeritz & Co.'s book was assembled with brass fasteners and allowed for additions and deletions. Although their address is New York, all their labels were printed in Germany.

23.

26.

25.

27.

28.

22.

Variations

In almost every field of non-contrived collectibles, variations in the product inevitably occur due to a variety of unplanned circumstances. In the coin world, you have a plethora of variations, from different mint marks to added tail feathers in eagles. In the art world, you can find hand-colored, first-edition Audubon birds or chromolitho second editions. The McKenney-Hall Indians were produced by three different publishers, and Pocahontas looks like she put on 40 pounds in one of the variations.

The very nature of the cigar industry at the turn of the century created a scenario that undoubtedly produced an unlimited number of variations. Here was an industry of over 100,000 cigar manufacturers, ranging from the largest with hundreds of employees to small, mom & pop "Buckeye" factories that existed across the countryside.

Add to that scenario an army of lithographers offering thousands of sample images, including blank "stock" labels so that cigar makers could drop in any message or custom artwork they desired. In their pleas for business, many lithographers stated emphatically, either in their correspondence or right on the samples, that they could make any changes the customer desired.

Under these conditions, which we know to be historical fact, the potential for variations has to be mind-boggling.

Many cigar makers had to "update" the image used on the label of a successful brand, so you may find changes in fashion or hairstyle, or horses and buggies replaced by automobiles.

So why haven't more variations surfaced to date? The logical explanation — which makes many of us cringe — is what we have learned from some of the old-timers that we interviewed. Quite simply, many product samples were destroyed, and for a variety of reasons that made sense at the time — changes of image, the need for space, fire, earthquakes, or in some cases, business failure. This is just another reason why we should appreciate and treasure those examples that did survive.

1. *Red Cap.* Both Heffron & Phelps and O. L. Schwencke produced this title in the late 1800s. In both cases, the title was part of the original art.

2. *Chic.* In both of these images the title was applied by letterpress, so the possibility exists that you could find the same images with different titles.
3. *True Blue / Elsedor.* American Litho produced this image in proof and sample form under the title of *True Blue*. Evidently, this customer requested the title *Elsedor* and absorbed the great expense of changing the stones.
4. *Flor de Leon.* Produced by Calvert Litho, the Joplin, Missouri cigar maker obviously rejected the proof showing the lion to be unhappy with cigar smoke, and made Calvert's artists change his attitude.

2.

4.

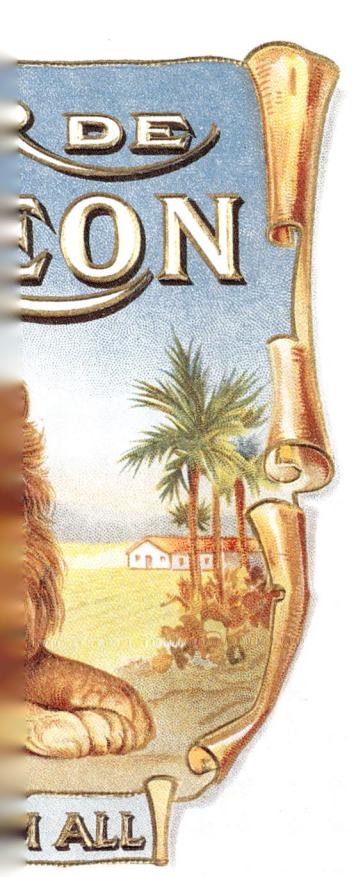

THE KING OF THEM ALL

5. *Upper Ten / Lord Coventry.* Originally offered in sample form by O. L. Schwencke as *Lord Coventry*, the identical image appeared with the letterpress title *Upper Ten*. By this time, O. L. Schwencke had been bought out by Moehle Litho.
6. *Cuban Heiress.* This stock label of a girl smoking, printed by Schlegel Litho, wound up carrying the title you see here. Not willing to settle for a letterpress title, the customer went to the extra expense of having it embossed in gold.
7. *Cremola de Cuma / Fabrica de Tabacos.* Produced in sample form by Klingenberg Litho as *Fabrica de Tabacos*, the customer went to the expense of changing the title on the stones.
8. *Bachelor Girl, Miami Club,* F. M. Howell, the label discounter from Elmira, New York — who supplied thousands of mom & pop cigar makers with cheap photomechanical labels — certainly had a winner in this young lady. Here are just two examples in which her image was used.
9. *Open Heart.* This unique fencing image by Calvert changed dramatically through the years. Many lithographers often updated the image of a successful brand.

5.

7.

8.

9.

6.

5. Classic Brands
American Classics

Sometimes called Americana, or "slice of life," one of the things that the American Classics have in common is their depiction of life as it was or as it should be, along with a sprinkling of patriotism, ethnicity, and an appeal to a variety of tastes. While some of the classic labels mentioned the fact that their tobacco was imported, the main message conveyed in many of the artworks was American ownership or American manufacture. This section covers the gamut, and we apologize in advance if we did not feature your favorite label.

1.

2.

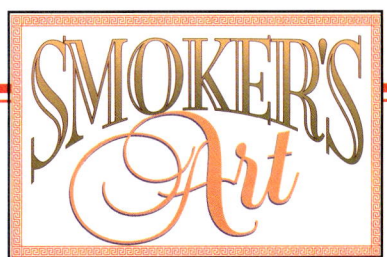

1. *America's Pride* * An outstanding and busy rendition of our first president, including the crossing of the Delaware.
2. *Artel De Luxe* * Good old Art Waegemans in Bridgeport, Connecticut decided the best way to reach his audience was to feature himself, just as today's car dealers appear on your television screen. He also covered all bases by displaying the Union bug to the right of his name.
3. *Black Bird* ***** A dapper fellow with a racing form.

4. *College Inn* ** A famous American brand name.
5. *Conewango* *** A Pennsylvania Indian canoeing on a lake.
6. *Don't* ***** A lady rejecting her dance partner's advances.
7. *El Biscayne* *** Miami scenes ("the world's winter playground").
8. *El Rosso* ** An Indian getting ready to mount his horse.
9. *Fifty Little Orphans* ** This George Harris artist squeezed in exactly fifty smiling young children to represent the fifty cigars in the box. Produced for the Joe Michl Cigar Company.

4.

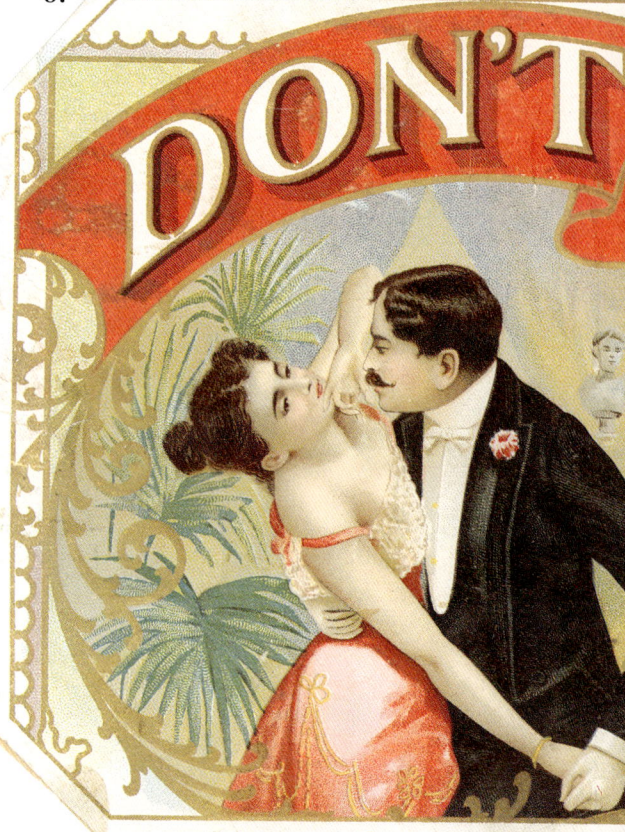

6.

5.

7.

8.

9.

10. *First Banner* ** George Washington, with a list of his "firsts."
11. *First Blush* ** Early Schlegel rendition showing the innocence of the time.
12. *First Cabinet* ** A fine rendition of Washington's Cabinet, including embossing, which gave the effect of canvas.
13. *Gay Boy* ***** A successful-appearing, turn-of-the-century lad.
14. *Gettysburg Commanders* *** A favorite label done by Globe Litho of New York, showing Hancock, Meade, and Reynolds.
15. *Hiawatha* ***** The legendary Longfellow hero, by Calvert Litho.
16. *Infallible* ** Certainly not the most modest claim, but this company had to set themselves apart from the competition.

13.

11.

10.

14.

12.

15.

17. *Iroquois* ***** Calvert Litho probably deserves a prize for producing the most spectacular Native American images.
18. *Jack Daniel* * Since cigars and whiskey usually went together in local taverns, the Jack Daniels Company had the Arturo Fuente Co. make a private brand just for them.
19. *La Zoos* *** This Kalamazoo, Michigan cigar maker created a tranquil theme with a name locals would identify with.
20. *Lincoln Highway* * A unique map, showing the famous U.S. Route 30 crossing the country.
21. *McCormick's Harvester* ***** This image was obviously produced to appeal to the large farming community. Cyrus McCormick patented the reaping machine in 1834 and died in 1884.
22. *Medal of Honor* ** Since medals and awards appeared on a large number of labels, this manufacturer chose the highest award possible for their brand.
23. *Medalist* *** Great gold leafing and embossing by this New York cigar maker, featuring the California seal.

19.

22.

23.

24. *Minnehaha* ***** The legendary Longfellow heroine, by Calvert Litho.
25. *Morning-Tap* ** The Seider Cigar Company chose a military wake-up theme featuring a cigar-smoking drummer.
26. *National Seal* ** A unique image featuring the seal of the Supreme Court of the United States.
27. *Nebraska Girl* *** A 1902 horsewoman in period costume.
28. *New Day* * Sunrise and sunset were always a good theme. J. J. McCauley & Sons from Uhrichsville, Ohio inserted a plantation into this art deco image.
29. *Nov. 11th Victory Day* * This cigar maker tried to capitalize on the armistice celebration at the end of World War I.

25.

26.

27.

28.

29.

24.

30. *Operator* ***** Telegraph operator was a highly respected profession in the 1890s.
31. *Our Pride* **** This cigar honored the opening of the Panama Canal. Maybe someone should create a cigar commemorating the fact we gave it away!
32. *Paid in Full* ** A popular brand, relating money to cigars.
33. *Pony Post* *** Much rarer than anyone imagined, these great examples of early western history virtually disappeared.
34. *Quaker Quality* ** Schlegel Litho produced this semi-textual showing a Quaker smoking and reading.
35. *Red Cloud* ** This important Sioux chief and orator probably never dressed like this. His name refers to the way in which his scarlet-blanketed warriors formerly covered hillsides like a red cloud.
36. *Sheboygan* ** This Wisconsin cigar maker combined great textual design with an Indian on the edge of a cliff.

31.

30.

32.

35.

34.

36.

33.

37. *Sioux* ** An Indian maid bringing home tobacco leaves.
38. *Susquehanna* *** Three Indian maidens graced the lid of this product from the Susquehanna Valley cigar maker.
39. *The Drummer* ***** A turn-of-the-century salesman giving his best pitch in the dining car!
40. *Toledo C. P. Squad* ***** Toledo Polish militia, known as the "Cherry Pickers Squad" because of their red uniforms. (The government was so paranoid, it made them dress in red uniforms for easy identification.)
41. *Tom Mix* ** The cowboy motion picture star (1880–1940). A social lion in Europe.
42. *Uncle Sam* *** Uncle Sam, created by Thomas Nast, was the ultimate symbol used by advertisers.

38.

37.

39.

41.

40.

42.

43. *War Cabinet* ***** President Lincoln meeting with his War Cabinet: Edwin M. Stanton, Salmon P. Chase, Gideon Welles, Caleb Smith, William H. Seward, Montgomery Blair, and Edward Bates. This rare image was produced by Calvert Litho.
44. *Winnie Winkle* **** Originally produced by Schlegel Litho and subsequently taken over by Consolidated Litho.
45. *Wizard* ** Coveted artwork, done by Schlegel Litho, featuring a wizard and cat.
46. *Untitled, Exposition* *** An Indian guarding the Pan-American Exposition in Buffalo, New York.
47. *Untitled, Indian chief* **** A portrait, with vignettes featuring smoking.
48. *Untitled, Indian hunter* *** A pose with bow and arrow. Sepiatone, with artist's signature.
49. *Untitled, Train* ** A period steam engine, with gold medals, cigars, and flowers.
50. *Untitled, Vanity label* ** Children or grandchildren were extremely popular as vanity subjects.

43.

45.

44.

48.

49.

50.

47.

46.

American Brands with an International Flavor

American pride notwithstanding, many American cigar makers, whether they were a large enterprise, with a factory and 100 hand rollers, or a mom & pop "Buckeye" from the hills of Ohio, felt that a certain international mystique was needed to sell their locally made cigars. Just as the early cigarette makers chose exotic Turkish and Egyptian themes, many cigar makers chose palm trees, plantations, foreign-looking characters, and island settings in an effort to add romance to their product. As with many of today's products, advertisers liked to tantalize the public appetite with the impression that they were purchasing a rare and exotic product from a faraway place.

There was obviously a natural tie-in, since the Spanish West Indies was the birthplace of the hand-rolled cigar. It was an accepted fact that some of the finest tobaccos came from the Spanish West Indies, and the use of a Spanish-sounding name implied to smokers that they were undoubtedly buying the best.

As domestically grown tobacco improved in quality and became more readily available at lower cost, many cigar makers began cutting costs by using domestic fillers combined with a clear Havana wrapper, or a variety of combinations. One of the best examples we can give you in this section is the beautiful and rare *La Flor de Romeo* — hand-rolled in New York by New Yorkers!

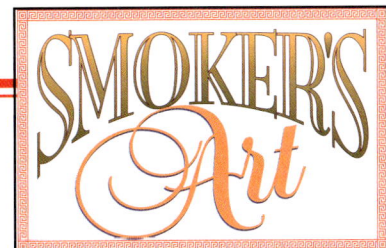

1.
2.
3.
4.

1. *A. Fuente* ** This famous brand featured the founder of this still popular and coveted brand.
2. *Amor y Zelo* * Man serenades girl.
3. *Artola* * A Grecian maiden honoring Olympian statue.
4. *Attracto* * Features a palatial mansion by a lake with swans.

5. *Corral de luxe* * Cuban tobacco. Tampa brand.
6. *Cuban Winner* A Cuban girl on a plantation.
7. *El Tolna* * Flor de Habana (*flower of Havana*), a Cuban beauty.
8. *Emilia Garcia* Girl in clouds holding cigar and orb.
9. *Empress of Cuba* ** A fictional empress. Tampa brand.
10. *Examiner* *** A Cuban man examining tobacco leaves.
11. *F. Lozano* * From the House of Morgan. Tampa brand.
12. *Flor de Cumbal* * Artist's creation of a coat of arms.
13. *Imperiales* ** Cavalier with shield.
14. *La Deliciosa* ** Crowned princess accepting cigars from Indian.
15. *La Exception de Casparino* * Monochrome image of Havana street scene.

9.

12.

10.

13.

14.

15.

16. *La Flor de Romeo* ** Great art, Spanish theme, American tobacco — and the label was made in Germany!
17. *La Granda* * Philadelphia brand with European coat of arms. Consolidated Litho.
18. *La Suprema* * A 1914 brand utilizing only three colors.
19. *La Triunity* ** Columbia on horseback with awards, plantations, and shipyards.
20. *Las Amantes* ** Grecian lovers (amantes = *the lovers*).
21. *Manila Blunts* * Indianapolis brand using some Philippine tobacco.
22. *Manila Stubs* * Indianapolis brand using some Philippine tobacco.
23. *Moro Light* * Although this famous Cuban lighthouse appears in hundreds of images, this brand makes it the main feature.
24. *Murona* *** Oversize label with girl and plantation house.

16.

17.

18.

24.

20.

23.

19.

22.

21.

25. *Nordacs* ** Scadron family name in reverse, featuring Norseman.
26. *Pasadena* ** Topless Indian with Cuban and American girls, Moro Light in background.
27. *Porto-Vana* * Havana–Puerto Rican blend of tobacco.
28. *R. Alvarez* * Frequently classified as a vanity label, this brand, produced by Mr. Alvarez, still maintained a Caribbean theme.
29. *Regreso* * Columbus, queen, Indians, Havana harbor.
30. *Ricaroma* ** Cuban lovers. Tampa brand.

25.

26.

27.

29.

28.

30.

31. *Rosa Mora* * Girl in portrait with lions. Havana tobacco. Tampa made.
32. *Triumphia* ** Girl with scales of justice, griffin, and capitol building in background.
33. *Webb's Tampa-Jewels* * Treasure chest on island beach. Drugstore brand.
34. *Untitled, Bearskin* *** Mediterranean girls on bearskin. American Litho.
35. *Untitled, Felicity* *** Lovers with Cupid.
36. *Untitled, Globe* *** American Litho prestigious brand. interpretation giving a global look.
37. *Untitled, Romance* ** American Litho rendition of colonial lovers.

37.

31.

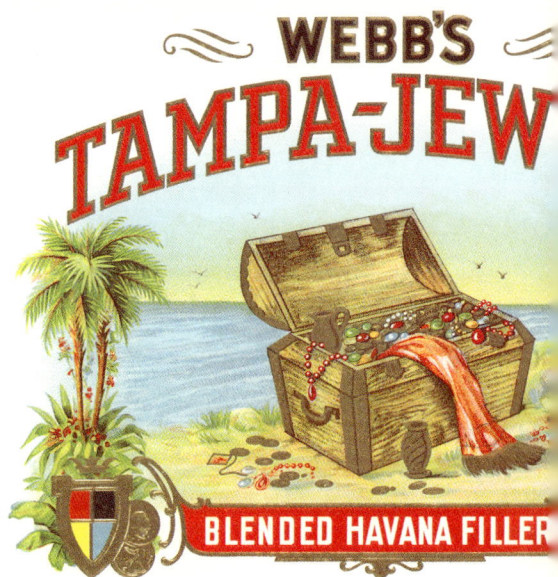

34.

33.

32.

TRIUMPHIA
MILD HAVANA BLEND

35.

36.

International Classics

Marketing is marketing, wherever you are located on this globe. Just as many American cigar makers attempted to depict American lifestyles or fantasies on their labels, the same approach applied worldwide. European cigar makers had the additional benefit of having some of the finest lithographers on earth right in their own back yard.

We now know that a rather large percentage of the labels produced by such lithographic giants as Klingenberg, Hermann Schött, and Weigang went to the U.S. market before World War I. Although this period was a slight setback for European lithographers, they had a ready and willing customer base in a number of other countries until they could resume selling in the U.S. in 1919.

We believe that credit should be given where credit is due. Here is one of those times. In 1991, Mr. A. DeLaet wrote a book called *Over Het Verzamelen van Sigarekistmerken*, which translates from the Dutch as *Concerning the Collection of Cigarbox Marks*. This book recognizes authors Joe Davidson and Tony Hyman for their work, but the remarkable thing about it is the time Mr. DeLaet put into listing all the foreign trademarks of the lithographers. A hand-drawn copy of the mark with the name, date, and city clearly gives the necessary information. Most European band collectors use this as their reference.

3.

1. *Ambu Gold* *   Roman and lion. H. Carl Bruning.
2. *Arethusa* ***   Nymph and satyr. Julius Jahl.
3. *Black-Watch* *****   The famous Scottish regiment.
4. *Bloemeke* ***   "Little Flower." Extremely ornate
5. *Bouddha* **   An image of "the enlightened one."
6. *Bouncer* *****   A French-Canadian manufacturer chose this theme.

1.

6.

4.

5.

2.

7. *Bugler* ***** The British loved military themes.
8. *Burgfeuer* ** European knight, burning castle. August Osterrieth.
9. *Fabriek van Sigaren* ** Label for oversize box of 200 or more with nautical theme, also titled *Mariner*.
10. *Fina* ** Unique silhouette of butler smoking;. Also titled *Siluetta*.
11. *Flor de Verano* *** "Flower of the summer." The good life in Europe. Klingenberg Litho.

11.

FLOR DE VERANO

9.

12. *Flor del Arte* ** "Flower of the Art." Pegasus and artists. Klingenberg Litho.
13. *Goethebund* *** Author and philosopher Wolfgang von Goethe. H. Conrad Deines.
14. *Gute Freunde* * Cigar-smoking hunter.
15. *Herzblättchen* * Children were a common theme everywhere. Moritz-Preschner.
16. *Hollandsche Sigaren* ** Label for oversize box of 200 or more with colonial theme.

13.

14.

16.

17. *International* *** Smokers of the world.
18. *Jucunda* *** Fairy-tale fantasy.
19. *Lekboot* ** Excursion paddle boat.
20. *L'Interallié* ** Allied Forces vs. Germany..
21. *Maaneklips* ** Unique Dutch subject, printed in Germany.
22. *Manobra* *** Excellent depiction of American Indian. H. Carl Bruning.

17.

19.

18.

21.

20.

22.

23. *Marokko* *** Cigars were a sign of success in Morocco also.
24. *Mi Flor Antonio Lopez* * Cuban brand for the national market. Heinrich Deussen.
25. *Mignon* *** Klingenberg artists captured the beauty and innocence of this sweet child in an effort to sell cigars.
26. *Moza de Fiesta* *** "Holiday Girl." Salome doing her famous dance. Klingenberg Litho.
27. *Nations Alliées* *** American, British, French, and Belgian allies.
28. *Negerköpp* ** "Black heads," by Hermann Schött.

23.

24.

25.

26.

27.

28.

29. *Papa* ***** Universal title.
30. *Peppi* *** This manufacturer felt that his cigars were so mild even Little "Peppi" could enjoy them. Moritz-Preschner.
31. *Pius X* ** Even a Pope made it to a cigar label. Hermann Schött.
32. *Preussenfunk* * Prussian eagle on thundercloud with lightning. Klingenberg Litho.
33. *Radiax* ** Diana the Huntress with golden bow. Hermann Schött.
34. *Radius* ** Mount Vesuvius is still on everyone's mind.

29.

30.

31.

32.

33.

34.

35. *Reform* ** Featuring women's liberation in Europe. Heinrich Deussen.
36. *Rothkäppchen* *** "Little Red Riding Hood." Here, she is about to enter her grandmother's house, with the wolf looking out of the window.
37. *Ruhm* *** "Glory." Beautiful statue by Moritz-Preschner.
38. *Schneidig* ** "Sassy." Girl bicyclists smoking.
39. *Torero* ** "Bullfighter."
40. *Victoria* ** This Caribbean maker relied on Hermann Schött Litho of Germany to create this image.

40.

35.

37.

38.

36.

39.

41. *Untitled* ** "Arco." Races of man, rainbow. Hermann Schött.
42. *Untitled* *** "Armada" ships sailing to the New World.
43. *Untitled* *** "Duett." Cigar-smoking dancing girls.
44. *Untitled* *** "Flor del Amor." Copied from famous painting of Cupid and Psyche. Produced by Klingenberg Litho.
45. *Untitled* *** "Germanicus." Roman warriors honoring the Emperor.
46. *Untitled* *** "La Vanidad." Art nouveau peacock.
47. *Untitled* ** "Teretto." Girls hiding smoking cigars behind their backs.
48. *Untitled* *** "Unitas." Columbia uniting "natives" and animals in the tropics.

41.

44.

42.

43.

47.

45.

45.

46.

48.

49. *Untitled* **** "Valkyrie." Mythological Valkyries taking fallen warrior to Valhalla.
50. *Untitled* **** Gnomes and toadstools. Wilhelm Wefers.
51. *Untitled* ** Kaiser Wilhelm II.
52. *Untitled* ** "Non Plus Ultra." America, Mexico, Germany, and Cuba featured. Klingenberg Litho.
53. *Untitled* ** Peasant girl looking at castle.
54. *Untitled* *** Sailor smoking. U.S. flag has stars of David. Klingenberg Litho.
55. *Untitled* **** Victorian lovers.

49.

54.

50.

51.

52.

53.

55.

Cuban Gold

"Cuban gold" is the term most commonly used in the cigar label collecting field to refer to the heavily gilded labels produced by and for the Cuban cigar industry. Coveted by most collectors and historians, they are also quite rare compared to those printed in the United States. In fact, over 90% of those that have surfaced exist in quantities of less than 100! There are a number of theories why so few have survived, ranging from rumors that Fidel Castro sold them to Spanish collectors in the late 1950s, to the possibility that Cuban cigar manufacturers were much more conservative than U.S. cigar makers and ordered labels in much smaller quantities from the lithographers — due in part to high printing costs.

What Cuban cigar makers did learn from their American competitors was that they needed the most spectacular, eye-catching images imaginable in order to attract the attention of potential customers. While American cigar makers opted for more "folksy" images on their labels and were not as concerned about gilding, Cuban cigar makers gave a much richer appearance to their labels by using more and more pure gold-leaf embossing, which would jump right out when the customer surveyed the cigar case. What is also interesting is that they usually tried to combine the rich and regal appearance of their labels with scenes that showed an exotic "Caribbean" look.

Evidently, Cuban lithographers could not completely satisfy their customers' needs and desires, so cigar manufacturers began to search the world over for the very best artisans — and they found them in Germany, the birthplace of stone lithography. While most German lithographers of the time exhibited superior workmanship, the masters of heavy gilding and embossing were Hermann Schött Co. and Gebrüder Klingenberg (Klingenberg Brothers) — which probably explains why many of the labels produced for Cuban cigars carry their trademarks.

No matter whether you choose to specialize by lithographer, subject matter, or historical period, we feel that no collection would be complete without at least a few examples of "Cuban Gold."

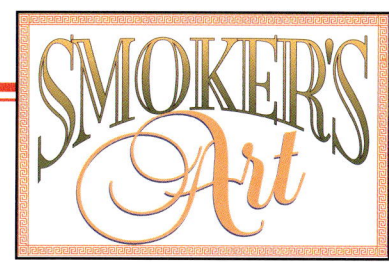

106   CLASSIC BRANDS • *Cuban Gold*

1. *Aspallo* *** Although the maiden in the troika dominates this scene, Klingenberg artists had to include the Moro lighthouse and palm trees.
2. *Club Royal* ** This grand Victorian building flying American flags was produced by Klingenberg. The title *Club Royal* and the glowing claims about their product in Spanish were printed later by letterpress, indicating that this was a stock label.
3. *Fabrica de Tabacos Primeros* *** Using Bartolozzi-type cherubs holding coats of arms, the lithographer surrounded the Cuban Bay scene with over twenty gold medals.
4. *Flor de Cielo* *** Klingenberg artists attempted to attach a heavenly quality to this brand.
5. *Flor de Rivero* * Plantation scene and Señor Rivero done by Klingenberg.
6. *Flor de Rosas* *** Typical Klingenberg art featuring Victorian costume, heavy gold leaf, and beautiful flowers.

1.

4.

2.

5.

ELO

3.

FABRICA DE TABACOS
PRIMEROS

E RIVERO

7. *Flor El Todo* *** One of the earliest embossed labels done for the Cuban cigar makers, the lithographer at Hermann Schött gilded every available square inch!
8. *Gran Marca de Cigarros* ** By lithographers Kunstanst, Ferd., Wefers & F. Audiger in Kempen, Germany. Pretty girls in mantillas were commonplace on many labels, but in this instance, the girl is smoking.
9. *La Confederacion Suiza* *** Printed in Cuba, these labels were discovered in Tampa, Florida. This is one of the few examples where Cuban Lithographers attempted to duplicate their German counterparts' heavy gilding and embossing.
10. *La Flor de Cremava* ** Typical Klingenberg image, incorporating girls, clouds, medals, and tobacco plants.
11. *La Flor de la Vuelta* ** This artist tried to cover all the bases, including Indians, a queen with the Cuban coat of arms, a "dandy" smoking a cigar, and a harem girl with a water pipe.
12. *La Gira* *** An excellent example of Hermann Schött's heavy gilding and crisp embossing.

10.

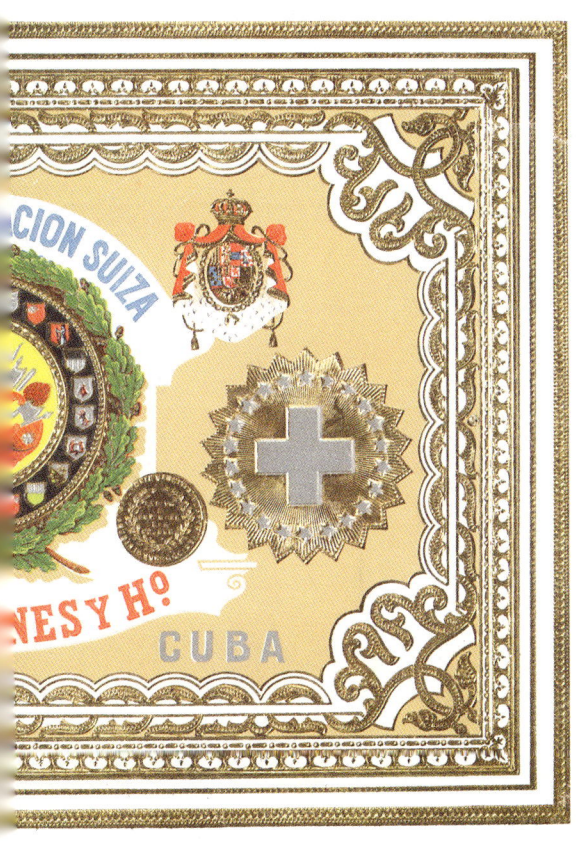

12.

13. *La Nativa Habana* ** A typical pre-gilding-era image, circa 1880, featuring medals won in London, Paris, and Vienna from 1855–1873.
14. *La Perla Habana* ***** "The pearl of Havana." A rare and extremely coveted example produced by the Heinrich Deussen Co. in Germany.
15. *Maradas* *** Produced by the master lithographer Hermann Schött. This artwork combines native Americans with trains, ships, and gold medals to imply that they were "global."
16. *Marca Preferida* ** This unique Klingenberg image features the island of Cuba in a blue-green sea surrounded by over thirty gold medals.
17. *Perla del Mar* * A post-World-War-I brand, printed in Cuba by Compañía de Litográfica de la Habana, but discovered in Tampa, Florida.

13.

15.

16.

17.

14.

18. *Rosa de Santos* **** One of the most spectacular pieces of artwork produced by Klingenberg Litho. Their lithographer's ability to simulate the glowing match illuminating the girl's face is equal to any artwork done in oils. They also had a penchant for heavy gilding and beautiful flowers. This brand also sold in the U.S. market under the name *Hazel Kirke*.
19. *Saluta* * Cuban banner surrounded by waves. Klingenberg.
20. *Verdier* ** Printed in Cuba by Compañía de Litográfica de la Habana. This brand was directed at the U.S. market.
21. *Untitled, Cuban gold* *** Female warrior, rainbow, Cuban flags. Copyright by American Litho along with a German Dep (trademark) number.
22. *Untitled, Girl Smoking Pera* *** In an effort to promote or justify women smoking cigars, this cigar maker featured an aristocratic-looking young lady in a Caribbean seaport. Done by Hermann Schött.

20.

19.

22.

21.

18.

23. *Untitled, Gran Fabrica de Tabacos* ** Heavy gold leaf, banners, crests, and sailing ships. Produced by Klingenberg.
24. *Untitled, Bella Cubana* ** Done by the Paul I. Landsman Co. of Mannheim, Germany. This Indian maiden is surrounded by all the basic trappings to satisfy the Cuban cigar maker, including the Moro Light, plantation workers, and of course, flowers and heavy gold leaf.
25. *Untitled, Native offering golden ship* **** Although the lithographer is unknown, it appears to be vintage Klingenberg or Schött. Whoever printed it, it is spectacular artwork.
26. *Untitled, Non Plus Ultra / La Flor de Cocosa* *** This oversize image, probably produced for a box of 250 or 100 presidente size, displays the best workmanship of Klingenberg, along with a patriotic Cuban theme.

24.

26.

23.

25.

6. Classic Themes
Famous Men

When the art of stone lithography was at its peak at the turn of the century, the list of subjects available to adorn the tobacco industry's packaging seemed almost endless. Famous men were an easy choice, since most of them had already been drawn and immortalized in history books and biographical encyclopedias.

Although generals, war heroes, and conquerors were an easy choice for the lithographic artist, men of the arts, writers, poets, philosophers, painters, and theater performers also lent their names and faces to the promotion of tobacco products.

Historians now believe that many important contributors to our history would be lost in obscurity, were it not for the fact that their images were used to promote a variety of products. One example would be the Spanish explorer Martin Pinzon, whose likeness appears on the *Navigator* label. Given command of the *Pinta* — his brother Francisco was the ship's pilot, and his brother Vincente commanded the *Niña* — Martin Pinzon's suggestion to change course on October 7, 1492 brought the fleet its first sight of land on October 12th.

In November of 1492, Pinzon and the *Pinta* went searching for gold and spices and discovered the island of Hispaniola (now Haiti and the Dominican Republic). Pinzon rejoined the fleet in January, 1493 for the return voyage to Spain, but was again separated from it by storms. No one knows whether Pinzon hoped to claim credit for all the discoveries by trying to reach Spain before Columbus, or whether he believed Columbus and the Santa Maria had been lost at sea. In any case, Columbus received a hero's welcome when he arrived back in Spain and Pinzon died shortly thereafter, remembered primarily for his supposed disloyalty.

Fame was even more fleeting in the entertainment world. For example, Clint Ford was a versatile

9.

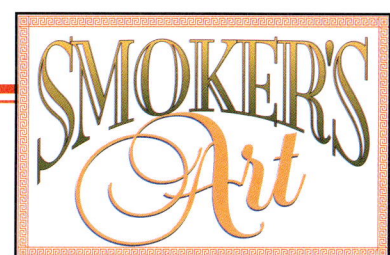

actor who played in New York theaters during the latter half of the 19th century. His versatility as an actor landed him numerous starring roles, yet today his name is no longer recognized.

The label titled *Master Diver* was a mystery for a long time. We spent hours, even days, researching this image. One fellow collector tried to convince us it had to be from Jules Verne's *Twenty Thousand Leagues Under the Sea.* The argument seemed logical. Then, out of the blue, Jake Rosenfield, from the Five-Cent Cigar Company, shared the following informational plum with us. When the Race Rock Lighthouse in New York was finished in 1878, a best-selling book, *Caleb West: Master Diver,* was written by the project engineer. The smiling gentleman featured on the cigar label was Caleb West! Jake was also able to explain both of the vignettes. (Jake sells a great T-shirt with the reproduced label image, and his research is included on the box the shirt comes in.) Once you discover this kind of historical information, you can't help appreciating the image even more.

Whether the subjects are famous or not-so-famous today, the historical interest alone contributes dramatically to the enjoyment of owning and researching the individuals who are featured on cigar labels. Who knows, maybe you'll discover a James Smithson label somewhere and the owner won't know or care who he is!

CLASSIC THEMES • *Famous Men*

1. *Bering* ** Danish navigator employed by the Russians to discover whether Asia and North America were connected. He died on the island named for him.
2. *Bret Harte* *** The American writer (1836-1902) and typesetter of San Francisco.
3. *Cervantes* ** Spanish novelist and author of *Don Quixote*.
4. *Champ Clark* * American political leader (1850–1921) and prominent presidential candidate (Dem.) of 1912. Speaker of the House 1911–19.
5. *Clint Ford* * A 19th-century stage actor.

1.

2.

3.
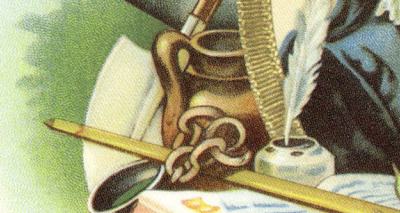

5.

CLINT FORD

By Permission

CHAMP CLARK

4.

6. *Columbus* ∗∗∗ Columbus pointing to land.
7. *Damasco* ∗ Nobleman done by Pasbach-Voice Litho.
8. *Don Alasco* ∗ Spanish nobleman.
9. *El Ministro* ∗∗ Winston Churchill, the ultimate smoker. (see page 117)
10. *Fellow Citizens* ∗∗∗ An outstanding rendition of the commanding generals (Lee and Grant) of the Civil War, produced by Calvert Litho.
11. *Ferdinand de Alba* ∗∗ The duke of Alba, Spanish general and regent of the Spanish Netherlands.

7.

6.

8.

9.

11.

12. *Flor de Mañuel* * Manuel I, king of Portugal during its "Golden Age."
13. *Franklin D. Roosevelt* * America's 32nd president (Democrat). Campaign image for political gifts.
14. *General Almonte* ** Mexican general and statesman (1804–1869) who tried twice for the presidency.
15. *Henry Clews* ** Banker and broker (1834–1923), one of the agents of the U.S. government in marketing bonds to finance the Civil War.
16. *Irish Singer* ** Denis O'Sullivan, famous Irish actor and singer born in San Francisco.
17. *Irvin S. Cobb* * American journalist, humorist, dramatic writer; his autobiography, *Exit Laughing,* was published in 1941.

12.

13.

14.

15.

16.

"FAMOUS IRISH ACTOR & SINGER, BORN IN SAN FRANCISCO, 1868"

17.

18. *Izaak Walton* *   English biographer (1593–1683) and author of *The Compleat Angler*.
19. *James W. Scott* **   Famous Chicago publisher.
20. *John Adams* *   America's second president.
21. *John C. Calhoun* ***   American statesman. A graduate of Yale, member of Monroe's cabinet, and vice-president under John Q. Adams and Jackson.
22. *John Metaxas* *   Greek general and statesman (1871–1941). Dictator of Greece, 1936–41.
23. *Judge Wright* **   Possibly a genuine judge from Ohio or Michigan.

20.

18.

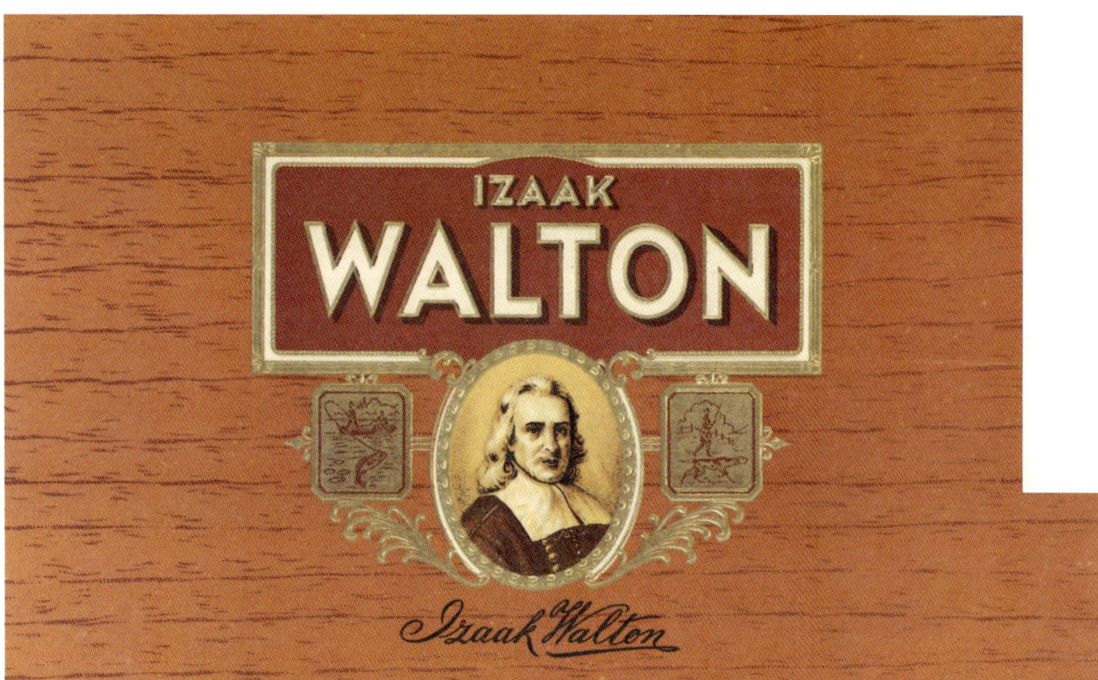

19.

22.

21.

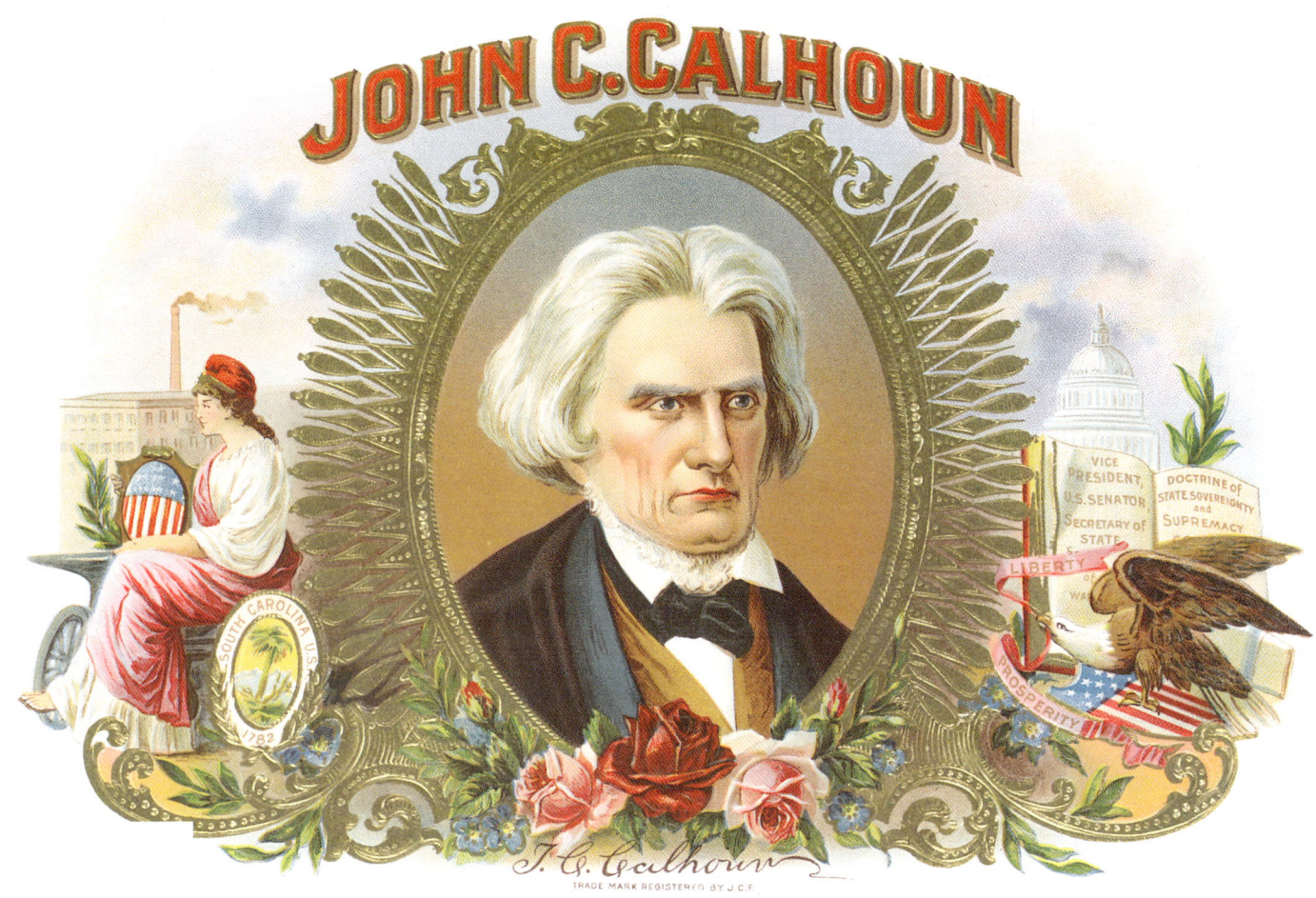

23.

126 CLASSIC THEMES • *Famous Men*

24. *Justin S. Morrill* **** Founder of the Republican party and Senator from Vermont, 1855-1890.
25. *King Carlos* ** Former king of Spain.
26. *La Flor de Lincoln* ** "Flower of Lincoln." An early Lincoln rendition.
27. *Lafayette* * French marquis, statesman, and officer. In 1777, he entered American service in the Revolutionary War. Close associate of George Washington.
28. *Lord Colbeck* ** English lord.
29. *Lord Curzon* ** Viceroy of India 1899–1905, authored *Lord Curzon in India* (1906).

24.

27.

26.

28.

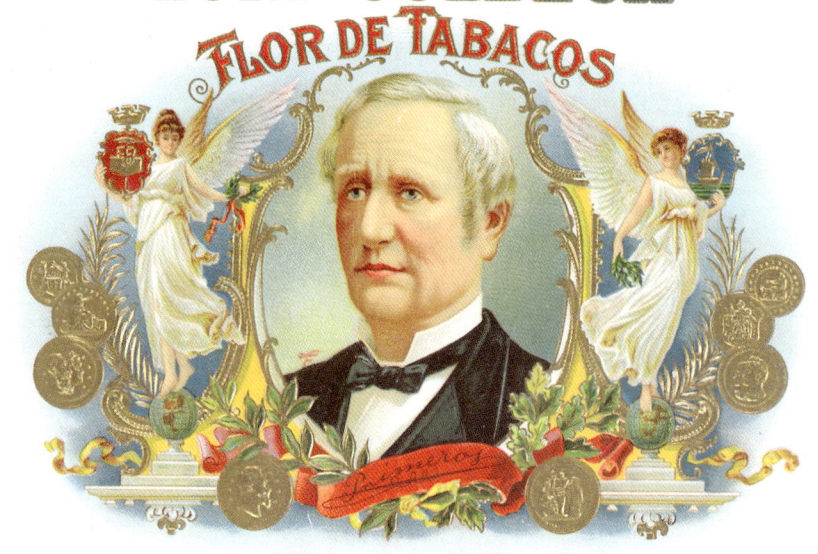

29.

25.

30. *Lord Romeo* ** Cuban nobleman.
31. *Marshall Field* * The man (1834–1906) who established the largest wholesale and retail dry goods establishment in the world.
32. *Monroe Doctrine* ** America's fifth president. Monroe was responsible for the Louisiana Purchase and the foreign policy referred to in this brand name.
33. *Navigator* **. Martin Pinzon, Captain of the *Pinta* during Columbus's voyage to the New World.
34. *Oliver Perry* ** Hero of the Battle of Lake Erie in the War of 1812, in which the British were defeated.
35. *Protector* ** Generalissimo Franco of Spain.

33.

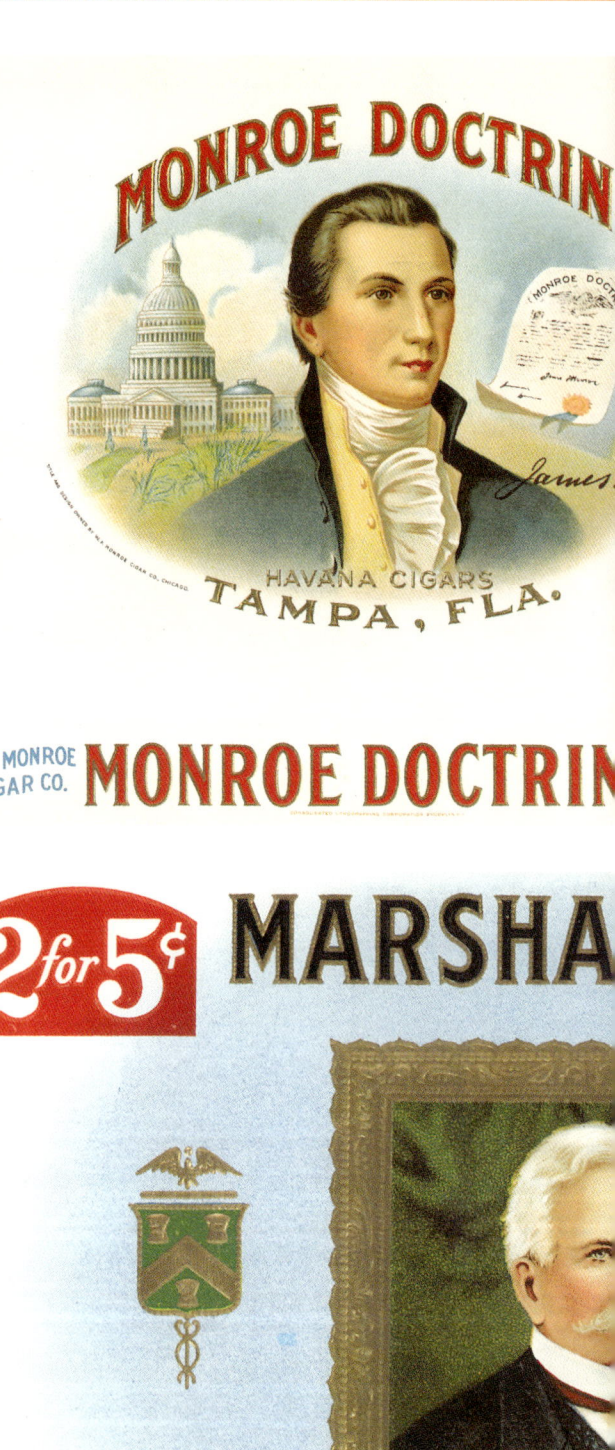

31.

32.

30.

34.

35.

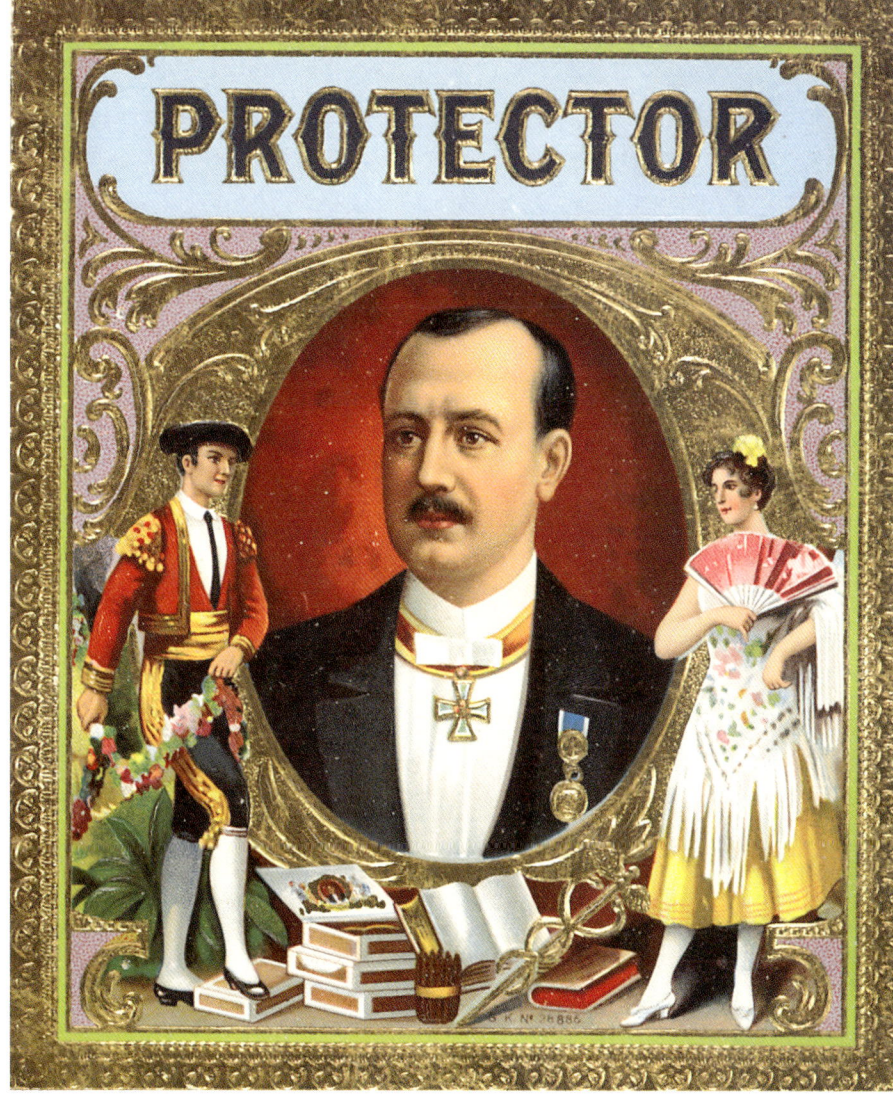

36. *Quelus* ∗∗∗ A Roman senator.
37. *Remus* ∗∗ Legendary founder of Rome, raised by wolves with his brother Romulus.
38. *Robert Peal* ∗∗ British lawmaker and founder of the "bobbies."
39. *Thomas Neale* ∗∗ Colonial postmaster in the reign of King William III.
40. *Vasa* ∗∗ Dynasty of Swedish kings (1523–1654).
41. *Wolfgang von Göthe* ∗∗ German philosopher, writer, and genius.
42. *Untitled, Royalty* ∗∗ A British king. Harris Litho.

40.

36.

42.

37.

38.

41.

39.

132 CLASSIC THEMES • *Famous Men*

43. *Voyager* ∗∗∗ Explorer, John Cabot.
44. *Genius*∗∗∗ Friedrich von Schiller, dramatist, poet, historian, and one of the greatest German literary figures after Goethe.
45. *Untitled* ∗∗∗ "Superbus," a Middle-East warrior.
46. *Untitled* ∗∗∗ Napoleon image in gold and sepia by Klingenberg.
47. *Untitled* ∗∗∗ Napoleon with Legion of Honor, by Hermann Schött.
48. *Untitled* ∗∗ Roman warrior.
49. *Untitled* ∗∗ William Taft, 27th president (Republican).
50. *Untitled* ∗∗ Woodrow Wilson, 28th president (Democrat).

45.

46.

48.

50.

44.

133

47.

49.

43.

Famous Women

Considering their customers were over 90% males, lithographers and tobacco manufacturers created images of things that men liked. Subjects such as sports, recreation, animals, exotic places, and war heroes were reasonably popular, but you can't fight nature, and what men seemed to appreciate as much as a good cigar or chew was women! Women of all ages, physical appearances, and stages of dress and undress appeared on labels. While some labels pictured women bare-breasted or in various stages of undress, such brands were usually found only in private men's clubs and pool halls.

Tantalizing and risqué as these images must have appeared in the 19th century, lithographers soon realized that the marrying kind of woman these men desired must appear pure, chaste, and rather demure. Although beauty is in the eyes of the beholder, the majority of females that appear on labels do fit that description.

With regard to levels of fame, we probably will never know why Schlegel Litho produced a label featuring Lady Curzon, wife of the Viceroy of India, unless it was to be sold as a companion to the one featuring her husband, Lord Curzon. Although a few hundred *Lord Curzon* labels surfaced in the 1970s, the only *Lady Curzon* images discovered came from the files of Schlegel Litho, and it is possible these labels never went into production.

While girls in "tomboy" dress appeared occasionally on labels, the most beautiful and classy tomboy, who always appeared quite feminine — even in her pilot suit (which she designed herself) — was Harriet Quimby. Even the most chauvinistic male cigar smoker must have admired not only her good looks, but also her impressive list of accomplishments, despite her short lifetime. Unfortunately, very few labels featuring her likeness have survived.

Regardless of their degree of fame, the women who appeared on the following labels are now etched in history.

Angela

1.

COPYRIGHT, BY AMERICAN LITHOGRAPHIC CO. NY   DEP Nº 3200.

CLASSIC THEMES • *Famous Women*

1. *Angela* **   A sweet young girl with a popular Victorian name. American Litho.
2. *Corona de Rosas* *   The St. Joseph, Missouri distributor commissioned O.L.Schwencke to create this worshipful image.
3. *Du Barry* **   Jose Alvarez chose Madame du Barry (1743–93) as the name of this brand. She was the mistress of Louis XV and was guillotined in the French Revolution.
4. *Hollandina* *   An American brand featuring a Dutch girl.
5. *La Belle Créole* ***   Featuring Fanny Davenport, who acted in Augustin Daly's theater company.
6. *La Coquette* ***   Pretty girl with cherries in her mouth and on her hat; also titled *Cherry Ripe*.

2.

4.

3.

5.

6.

7. *La Cornelia* * A Pennsylvania brand honoring a European countess.
8. *La Grande* ** A classy lady with regal trappings.
9. *Lady Curzon* **** Mary Leiter Curzon (1870–1906), American heiress, born in Chicago, and the financial support for her husband's political career.
10. *Lady Mary* * Victorian lady in plumed hat.
11. *Lillian Ashley* * An American actress.
12. *Marca Fina* ** "Concerto", Cuban guitarist.

7.

9.

12.

10.

11.

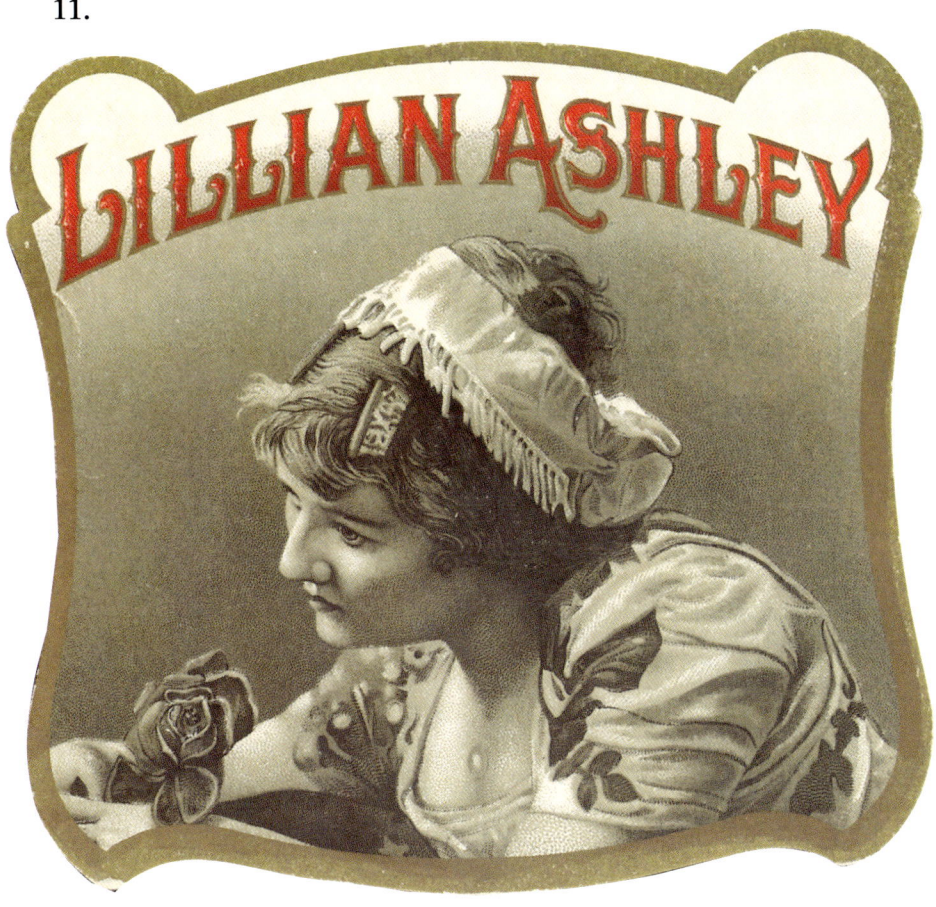

8.

13. *Marie Antoinette* ** Queen of France (1755–93), married to Louis XVI; unpopular for her love of luxury and indifference to the misery of the lower classes. Found guilty of treason and guillotined.
14. *O-Claire* ** A beautiful brunette, touting the perfect cigar.
15. *Silvia* *** Anyone named Silvia would love to identify with this regal beauty.
16. *Tobacco Girl* ***** "Coming through with the goods." Great artwork and humor by Schlegel Litho.
17. *Tungsten* **** "The brightest light in the cigar world." This brand capitalized on the recent invention of the electric light. Originally produced by Calvert Litho for the Wm. Stickney Cigar Company of St. Louis, it subsequently was transferred to Schlegel Litho and then to the William Steiner Company.
18. *Untitled* * "Carola," An innocent girl with long braids

13.

17.

18.

14.

16.

15.

CLASSIC THEMES • *Famous Women*

19. *Untitled* ** "Cubana." Cuban dancing girl
20. *Untitled* ** "Flor de Martina." Beautiful girl with flowers and waterfall.
21. *Untitled* ** "Mercedes." Stylish Victorian girl
22. *Untitled* ** "Parisette." Victorian girl in large hat.
23. *Untitled* *** "Purity." An innocent girl in plumed hat. American Litho.

21.

20.

23.

19.

22.

24. *Untitled* *** "Tokio." The American Litho artist gave Caucasian features to this Japanese girl.
25. *Untitled* ** "Tullia." A draped beauty in marble garden.
26. *Untitled* ** A Caribbean Indian girl surrounded by cigars.
27. *Untitled* *** "Geisha" Japanese girl. Incorporates Japanese lanterns, a traditional junk, and a turn-of-the-century battleship.
28. *Untitled* *** Semi-nude admiring flowers.

24.

27.

25.

26.

28.

29. *Untitled* *** Smiling Indian maiden in full costume. American Litho.

30. *Untitled* ** Stock image of girl in mantilla produced by Geo. Schlegel Litho.

31. *Untitled* ***** "Pilota." This image features America's first aviatrix, Harriet Quimby (1875–1912).
This multi-talented young lady worked successfully as a photo journalist for *Leslie's* magazine, and was America's first female screenwriter, selling seven of her screenplays to movie director D. W. Griffith.
Her aeronautical credentials include:
- The first American woman licensed to fly an aeroplane (August 1, 1911);
- The first night flight by a woman (1911);
- Winner of the Nassau Blvd. Air Meet Endurance Race, 1911;
- First woman to pilot her own plane across the English Channel (April 16, 1912 ; Dover, England to Hardelot, France).

The plane was built by Louis Blériot, who had accomplished this feat in 1909.
Harriet died on July 1, 1912 when her Blériot monoplane crashed at an air show in Squantum, Mass.
This label is part of the permanent collection of the Smithsonian Air and Space Museum.

31.

29.

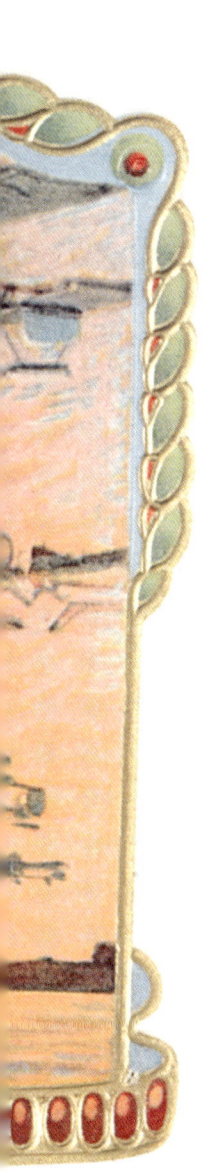

30.

Sports & Recreation

Sports and recreation were obviously fantasy themes, considering that they were produced at a time when a sixty-hour work week was commonplace. Rarely found in any quantity, their availability to cigar label collectors has been dramatically lessened because of their cross-collectibility. Whenever they appear at auction, sports and recreational images regularly set new price records, but the winners have historically been cross-over collectors, and not cigar label collectors.

1.

Red Stockings ***** An 1874 Boston brand

150 CLASSIC THEMES • *Sports and Recreation*

1. *Belle of the Rink* **** Victorian skaters by Schumacher & Ettlinger.
2. *Bowling Green* **** The early era of bowling.
3. *Caught On* ***** A couple fishing. (Look at the great moonlight on the water!)
4. *Checkers* *** Checkers players enjoying cigars.
5. *Crack Team* ***** No one will ever know for sure what message this Louis E. Neuman artist was trying to convey, but he obviously had a sense of humor.
6. *Fine Record* **** Trap and skeet shooting were popular pastimes for the élite at the turn of the century. The fact that the artist included a woman shooter in this scene was probably the prime attention-getter.
7. *Hand Made American League* ** The "straw poll" type of brand started with the first All-Star game in the 1930s.
8. *Hand Made National League* ** This "straw poll" type of brand matched its American League cousin.

5.

6.

3.

2.

4.

Title and Design Registered by ALFONSO RIOS & CO.

7.

Title and Design Registered by ALFONSO RIOS & CO.

8.

9. *Harry Pulliam* *** National League Commissioner (1910) who committed suicide. Also, the first Jewish Commissioner.
10. *Old Q* ** The Marquis of Queensbury, who established the rules of boxing in 1908.
11. *OleReb* * A hunter and his dog.
12. *Penalty* *** A goalie trying to block a penalty shot.
13. *Posish* ***** Pool players.
14. . (see page 149)
15. *Rich and Rare* **** Fly fishing was just as popular among the élite of the Victorian era as it is today. This early image says it all, according to O. L. Schwencke.

10.

9.

12.

11.

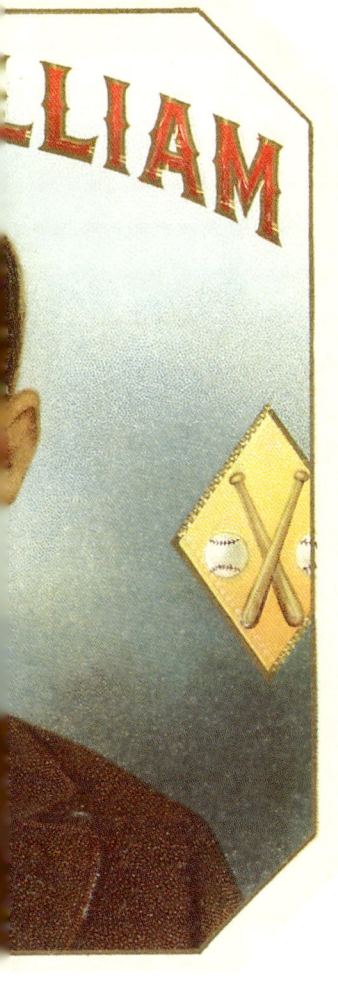

13.

15.

16. *Sport* ** Steeplechase racer.
17. *Sportwereld* *** Olympics, soccer, bicycling.
18. *Straight Hit* **** Early 1880s tennis.
19. *The Golf Club* ***** Early golfers teeing off.
20. *Ursus* ***** This rare Calvert image sold in 1996 for $1550. Bears fought bulls regularly in the Roman coliseum, but this rendition has a unique twist.

19.

17.

16.

18.

20.

156   CLASSIC THEMES • *Sports and Recreation*

21. *Y. H. P.* **** Yale, Harvard, and Princeton football. Done by Consolidated Litho, as well as Paul I. Landsman.
22. *Untitled* *** Fox hunter calling hounds. Gerhard Heymanns, Germany.
23. *Sport* **** Girl on skis.
24. *Untitled* *** A hunter relaxing with his dogs. Moritz Prescher.
25. *St. Huberto* ** St. Hubert, patron saint of hunters.

23.

25.

24.

21.

22.

Animals

Since the 13th century, animals have always been a favorite subject in the fine art world. Artists competed fiercely to capture and publish the most lifelike renditions of not only the animals that were familiar to the masses, but also the images of rare and exotic beasts from faraway places. As popular as such artwork was, even at the turn of the century animals were only occasionally used as the main theme for tobacco advertising. Other than the occasional dog or cat at the primary subject's side, a horse-racing scene to motivate the sports-minded smoker, or the subject riding a horse — which was the primary mode of transportation at the time — label artists relied primarily on scenes of either the Caribbean, men, women, or everyday life.

Whether lithographic artists were hard-pressed for new ideas or they finally realized that animal subjects in the fine art world sold well, they finally began to introduce and experiment with a variety of quadrupeds and winged creatures. Once they discovered that certain animals did have appeal, the more imaginative artists began to experiment, and started portraying animals in a variety of humorous themes such as *Cheese It* and *Haverkamp's Tiger Brand*.

Despite some degree of success, animals used as major themes captured a relatively small share of the tobacco advertising market. Once collectors began to realize this, animal subjects began to climb high on the asking list, and collectors soon discovered how rare they really were.

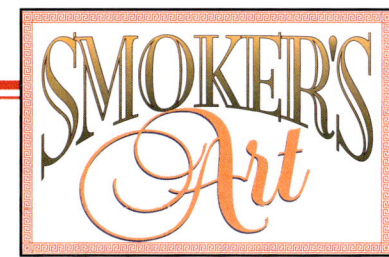

CLASSIC THEMES • *Animals*

1. *Alex* *   Black Scottie dog.
2. *Bald Eagle* **   A private brand for a grocery distributor.
3. *Black Bass* *   An early image done for Grauley Cigars.
4. *Cheese It* *****   Great art and humor combined by the Schumacher & Ettlinger artists.(*see page 159*)
5. *Condor* ***   Rare California bird.
6. *Durham Cigar* *****   Famous Durham bull.

5.

6.

7. *Gallus* ** Crowing rooster.
8. *Gopher* ***** Minnesota brand produced by Calvert Litho.
9. *Grand Lion* * Lion on globe.
10. *Haverkamp's Tiger Brand* **** Cartoon character tiger.
11. *Jbis* ** An ibis, the sacred bird of ancient Egypt.

8.

9.

7.

11.

10.

12. *Major Lark* *** "Still Marching On" evidently implied that this brand survived its competition.
13. *No Monkeying* *** Dogs playing cards and losing to monkey.
14. *Old Sport* **** French poodle with piercing eyes.
15. *Piet* ** Unique rendition showing a caged canary, which was quite a common household bird at the time because of its beautiful songs.
16. *Rex Aguilla* * King eagle produced by Schlegel Litho.

14.

165

13.

15.

16.

17. *Salamander* **** An unusual choice of subject, but maybe someone bought them.
18. *Swan* ** Swan in tropical setting.
19. *The Raven* * Raven perched on Poe's book of the same name.
20. *The Red Swan* ** Red swans feeding.

20.

17.

18.

19.

TITLE & DESIGN REGISTERED

168   CLASSIC THEMES • *Animals*

21. *White Cat* *   Popular title for a cigar in the 1920s. This is one of the rarest of all the White Cat brands.
22. *White Thief* **   Baby pig taking advantage of a free meal. Probably aimed at our large (at the time) rural population.
23. *Untitled, Deer* **   Deer at the edge of the forest.
24. *Untitled, Pointer* ***   Pointer with pheasant.
25. *Untitled, Winner* ***   Pigeon racing was extremely popular around the turn of the century.

24.

21.

22.  23.

169

25.

7. The Package Art Textuals

Sometimes called non-pictorial labels, cigar makers used textual labels about 20% of the time for a variety of reasons, the main one being their reduced cost. A number of small cigar makers who opted to invest their dollars in more costly tobacco rather than expensive artwork did develop a loyal clientele regionally, and relied on a textual image to get the job done.

Initially overlooked by some of the early collectors who were searching for eye-catching pictorial labels, textual images took a back seat for almost a decade until they started appearing at auction. Just as fine art dealers were attracted to the high-quality workmanship and multi-colored stone lithography of pictorial labels, graphic design artists and sign makers went wild over the unique designs on textual labels. It is rewarding to know that some of these imaginative designs are still appreciated and held in high esteem today.

1.

1. *American Gems* * An appeal to patriotism.
3. *Coca-Cola* *** In the 1940s, Coca-Cola licensed its name for use on chewing gum, candy, and cigars.

3.

2. *Bueno* * "Good" with a Spanish twist.
4. *Cosmopolitan Club* * Private club logo.
5. *Crown Cigar* * Ithaca, New York brand.
6. *Falcaro* ** Low-budget art for the bowler.
7. *Gagnon* * A French-Canadian brand with coat of arms.

2.

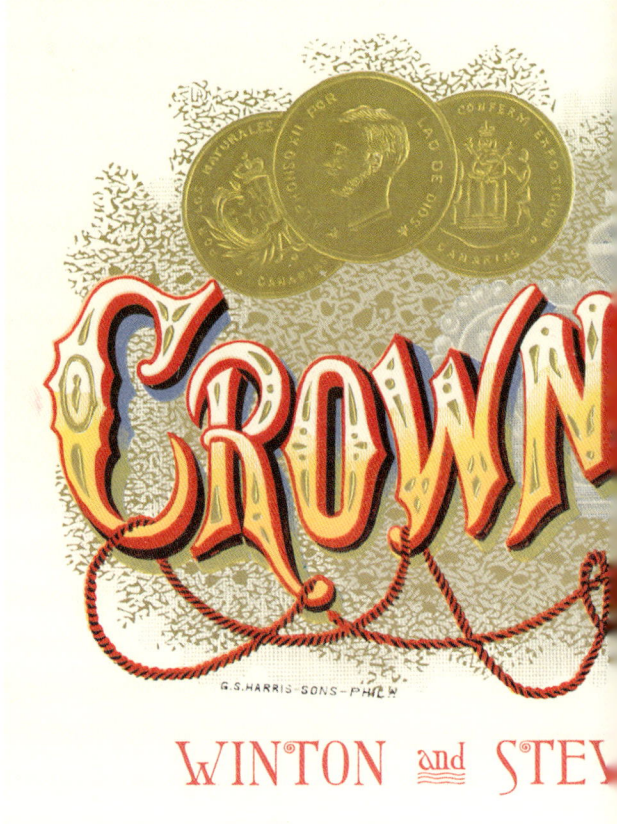

5.

4.

7.

6.

8. *Genteel* * An obvious appeal to refinement.
9. *Gold Dollar* ** We were still on the gold standard.
10. *Havana Smoker* ** Although Havana is in the title, they were probably made in Pennsylvania.
11. *La Docilla* * Tampa brand, ornate gilded border.
12. *La Flor de El Firma* * "The Flower of the Company." Textual, but a very busy design.

12.

8.

9.

10.

11.

13. *Old Seal* ** Incorporates a colonial wax seal.
14. *The Hustler* ** There were hustlers, even in Canada.
15. *Vinc-A-Cal* * California brand.
16. *World's Fair* * The 1938 World's Fair.

15.

14.

177

13.

16.

Copyright 1938 by Ellis B. Strickler

Trimmings

The term "trimmings" was used by the the cigar industry to describe all the ancillary pieces of artwork glued to either the inside or outside of the cigar box to complement the main 6 x 9 image printed on the inside lid. If the cigar maker could afford it, the lithographer continued the theme of the main image into all the trimmings. However, to help keep costs down, the small cigar maker could opt to use stock edgings and nail tags provided by the box maker.

In this section, we will show you each of the categories of trimmings by name so you may understand how each label fits into the big picture.

Although many advanced collectors try to find any or all of the trimmings as companions to their inner labels, their quest in many cases is in vain, since many of the items they seek were destroyed early on or ended up in flea market dealers' "junk packs."

The "junk packs" approach that has existed since the early 1980s was used by some dealers to unload images that could not sell on their own merit. While dealers would include a few decent images that showed in their ads, the majority were stock or blank images, along with miscellaneous flaps and nail tags. When you see an offer of 50 labels for $25, run for the hills. If it sounds too good to be true, it usually is.

2. *Aspallo* ** Cuban brand

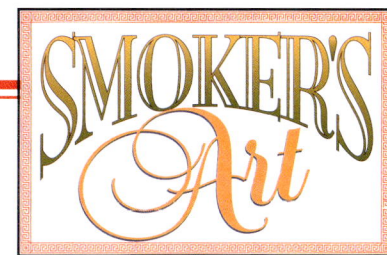

OUTER LABELS (100-Count Boxes)

Although they fall into the category of trimmings, the outer labels produced for boxes containing 100 cigars have now established their own niche in the art world. In the framing world, they are a definite competitor to their 6 x 9 inner-lid cousins.

Smaller than their 6 x 9 cousins, many outers still feature the same spectacular art in a more condensed format. Referred to in many cases as 4 x 4s or 5 x 5s, they were actually produced in a variety of sizes and shapes, including 4 x 6 rectangles, diamonds, squares, and hexagons.

Because of the smaller label size, lithographers could in many cases utilize the same stones used for the 6 x 9 inners, especially if the portrait or subject in the center of the 6 x 9 could fit into a 4 x 4 or 5 x 5 space. In some instances, this actually made the outer more attractive, and in others, you would need to see the inner to understand the theme or message the cigar maker (or artist) was trying to convey.

While there always has been a die-hard core of collectors who prefer the smaller-sized outer over the 6 x 9 inner, advanced collectors realized early on that in some cases only the outer has survived, just as you can often find only an inner or a flap. This phenomenon, or fact of life, was learned very quickly by collectors who wanted to complete "sets" — much to their dismay.

For many of the images featured here, an inner version can be found, but in many instances, the outer is the only example available. For example, when we found the *Double Elk* brand, there were over 500 inners, but fewer than 100 outers. That same ratio applies to many other brands you may be familiar with, such as *Los Inmortales* and *Pony Post.* For that matter, how many individuals own an outer for *Socrates, Magnolia, Red Bird* or *Maradas?* Interestingly, in some cases only the outer has survived, which is good news for the outer collectors, but frustrating for those who want to build complete sets.

In the 1980s, the 6 x 9 inner was still the most popular size among both collectors and retailers, who bought them for framing. In fact, there were very few collectors who specialized in collecting outers. By 1992, that picture had changed dramatically. At auction, some outers are now commanding higher prices than inners. In the framing world, three mail-order catalogs are offering beautifully framed outers exclusively.

The comparative rarity of larger outers can partially be attributed to the rise in popularity of 50-count boxes. After a short transition period, including the banding of the large outers so the retailer could identify them more easily on the shelf (see the *La Flor de Martinez* examples), they were eventually replaced by the familiar 2 x 5 outer labels.

1. *American Citizen* * Patriotic and union theme.
2. *Aspallo* .(see page 178)
3. *Bajazzo* * Jester and mirror.
4. *Bella Vista* ** "Beautiful Sight." The White House.
5. *Bertha* * Victorian theme.
6. *Black Crook* ***** Famous long-running New York play.

1.

3.

4.

5.

6.

7. *Clown* ***   A 19th-century artist's concept of a clown.
8. *Concerto* **   Cuban guitarist.
9. *Coronation* *   Coat of arms. S. S. Pierce Co., Boston.
10. *Cubana* *   Cuban dancing girl.
11. *El Poëta* **   Poe, Longfellow, Holmes, Goethe, and Schiller.
12. *Elsedor* **   Red-jacketed horsewoman.

8.

7.

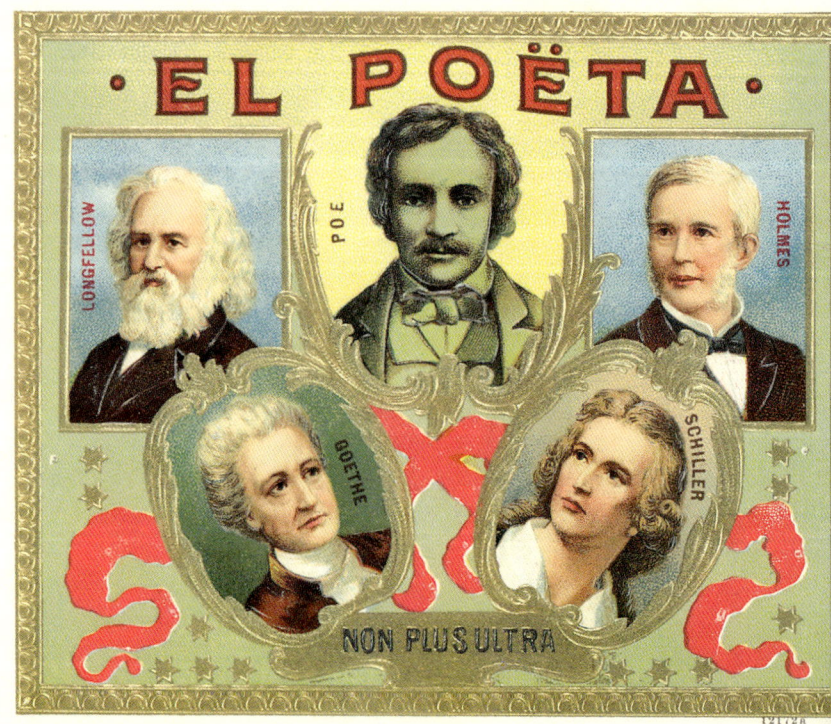

11.

10.

9.

12.

13. *Exposition* ** The Columbian Exposition of 1892.
14. *Felicity* ** A synonym for bliss and happiness.
15. *Flor de Alasso* ** Indians holding portrait.
16. *Flor de Habana* ** "Flower of Havana." Map of Cuba.
17. *Flor de Martina* * Typical 1890s heavy embossing. Large inner on page 143
18. *Flor del Canto* *** "Flower of Song."

13.

14.

15.

16.

18.

17.

19. *Grauley's* ** Private brand and logo.
20. *Heijene & Co.* ** Columbus landing.
21. *Heroica* ** Gladiator receiving award.
22. *Indiana* *** Indian brave with American flag.
23. *Jockey Club* * Jockeys and horse in the stretch.
24. *Joco* *** Black man smoking.
25. *Kensilla* ** Grecian theme.

20.

19.

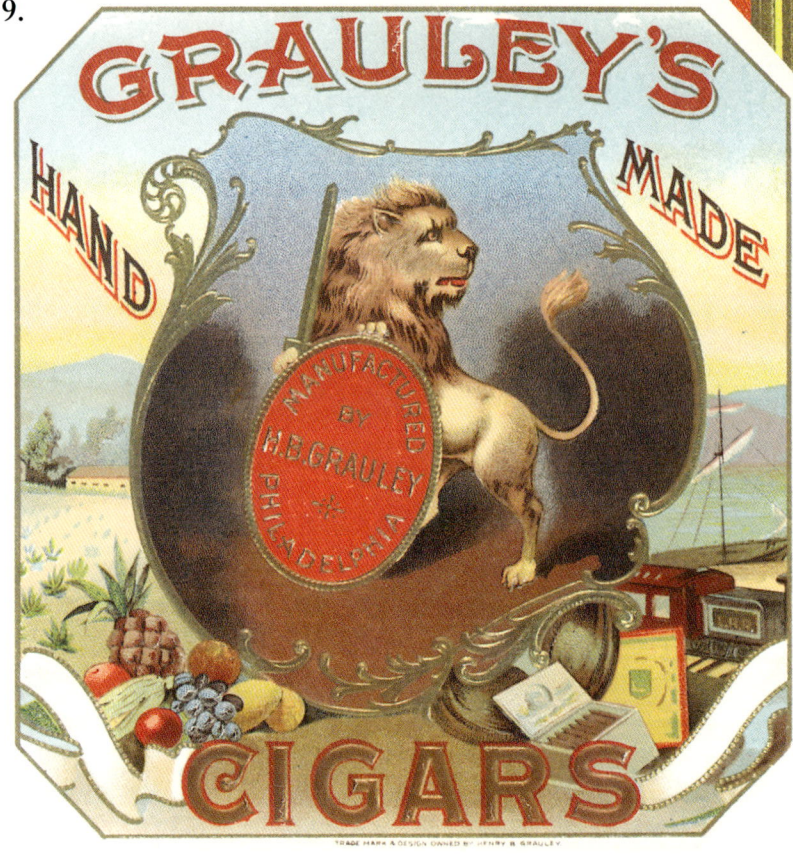

24.

22.

23.

21.

25.

26. *Keraco* ** Girl and cherub.
27. *Knickerbocker Club* * New York Knickerbocker smoking.
28. *La Flor de Cocosa* *** Cuban theme.
29. *La Flor de Luis Martinez* * Key West brand, early version.
30. *La Flor de Luis Martinez* * Key West brand, banded for box of 50.
31. *La Fuga* ** Indian maiden with American flag.
32. *Lector* *** Official reader for cigar rollers.

28.

26.

27.

30.

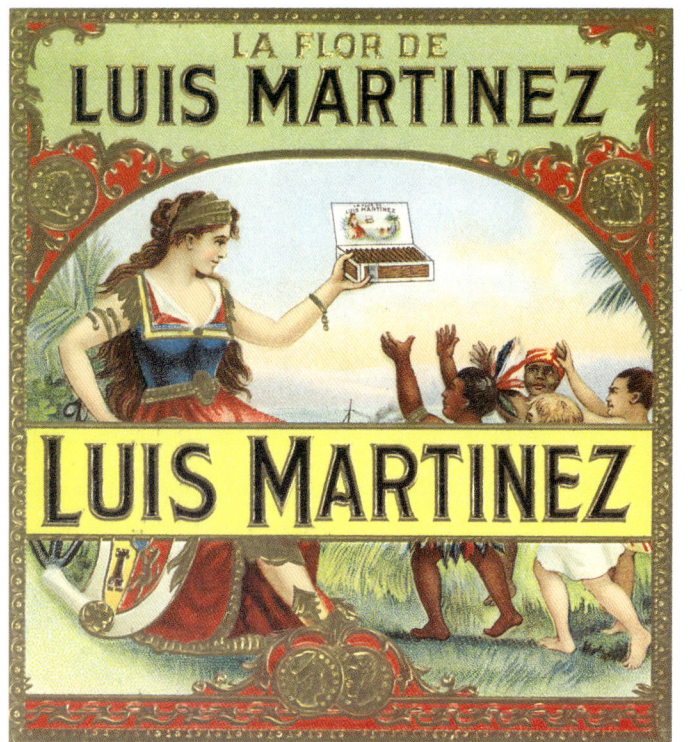

29.

31.

32.

33. *LuLu* *** Flapper girl with Black server.
34. *Mariner* ** A 19th-century sailor.
35. *Mefisto* ** An art nouveau devil.
36. *Partner* ** Earliest American Litho.
37. *Pengo* ** Black couple dancing.
38. *Presidentes* ** Cuban brand, American patriots.

33.

34.

36.

35.

38.

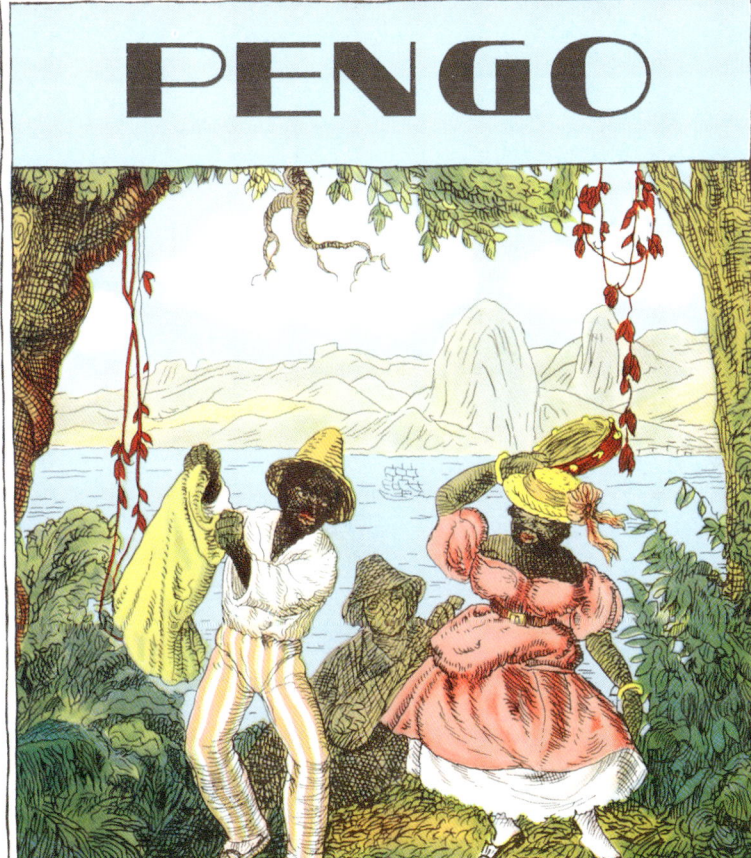

37.

THE PACKAGE ART • *Trimmings*

39. *Prize Solo* ***** Imaginative art by Witsch & Schmitt.
40. *Purity* ** Girl with innocent look.
41. *Red Bloomers* * Rose with woodgrain.
42. *Reunion* *** Night party scene.
43. *Rotten* **** Humorous attempt to sell this brand.
44. *Royal Opera* * Vienna scene.

39.

41.

40.

42.

43.

44.

45. *Selector* *   Cuban selecting tobacco leaves.
46. *Senta* **   Germanic princess. Wilhelm Wefers.
47. *Sport* ****   Young girl skier.
48. *Superbus* **   Artist's rendition of medieval warrior or leader.
49. *Surveyor* *   Washington at Mount Vernon.
50. *Tradition* ****   Royal greeting.

46.

47.

45.

48.

49.

50.

51. *Undertaker's Delight* ***** Prophetic image for cigar smokers.
52. *Union Eagle* ** Eagle over cigar factory.
53. *Unitas* *** International theme.
54. *Untitled, Santa & cherub* ** Santa & cherub toasting, 1884.
55. *Valenciana* *** Girl in ornate kimono smoking.

55.

52.

51.

53.

54.

56. *Valkyrie* *** Valkyries carrying warrior to Valhalla.
57. *Villa de Cuba* ** Early Tampa brand.
58. *Yankees* ** Uncle Sam dumping cigars.
59. *Yema* *** Art nouveau girls in smoke.
60. *Zepelina* **** Zeppelins were the new thing.

56.

57.

58.

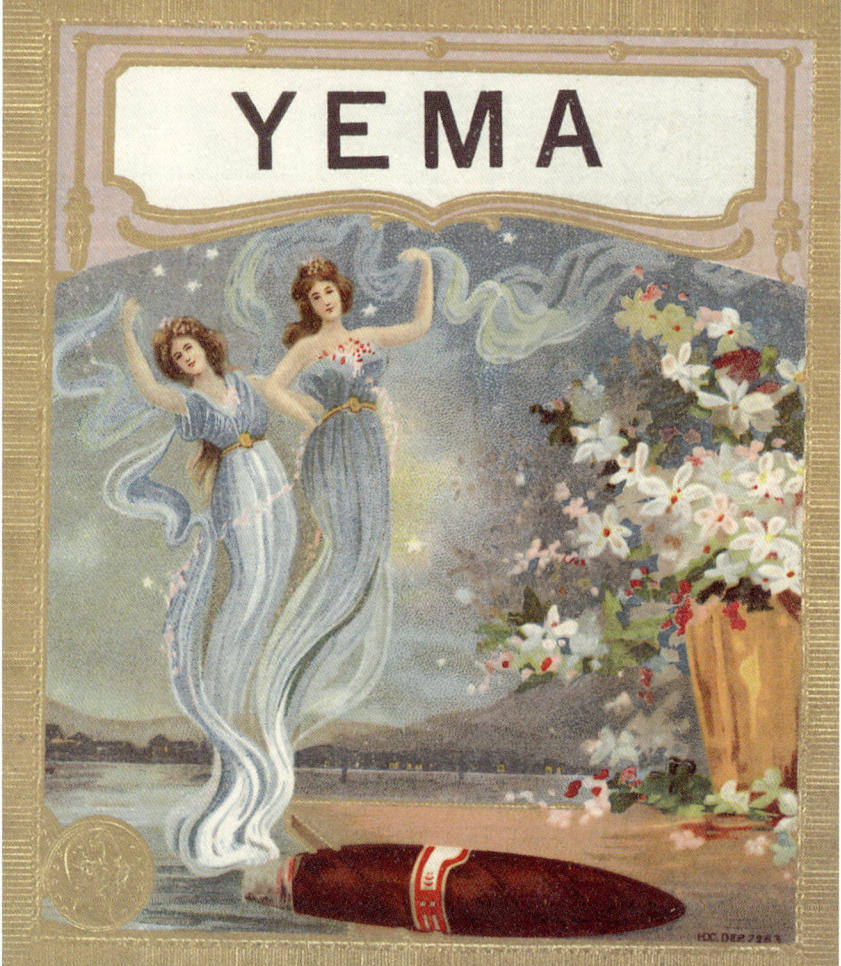

59.

1. *John Metaxas* * Greek president.
2. *Brick House* * Florida brand.
3. *White Orchid* * Popular Pennsylvania brand.
4. *Sun Beau* ** Western brand.
5. *Good Head* * Simple and to the point.
6. *Golden Lion* * Midwestern brand.
7. *El Florio* * Cuban theme.
8. *Slendorita* ** Strange nude cameo.

OUTER LABELS (50-Count Boxes)

The Federal Revenue Act of 1865 allowed cigars to be packed in quantities of 25, 50, 100, 250, and 500 cigars, but the most popular size until the turn of the century was the box of 100. The 100-count box usually had a 4.5 x 4.5 label on its side. During the rise in popularity of the 50-count box, cigar makers continued to use the 4.5 x 4.5 label by wrapping it over the edges. In some cases, this caused a problem for the retailer, who saw only a partial image — and no brand name — when boxes were stacked up and viewed from the side.

Before the introduction of smaller outers, lithographers introduced "banding," which was the addition of the brand name in the center of the 4.5 x 4.5 label.

By the time 50-count boxes became the number one seller, someone finally woke up and produced the easier-to-view 2 x 5 label, causing the demise of the 4.5 x 4.5 for boxes of 50.

1. *Thomas Neale* *   Supposedly, the first postmaster in the colonies in the reign of King William III.
2. *Javotte* *   A great addition to the ornate inner.
3. *Quaker Rose* **   Unique die-cut of the principal subject, obviously costly to produce.
4. *Untitled* *   Die-cut cavalier.
5. *The Old & The New* **   Unique early design.
6. *La Estrella de La Habana* *   Early diamond design.

OUTER OVALS

Larger than nail tags, the approximately 3 x 4 labels produced for the top of a wooden cigar box acted as a colorful replacement for the early method of "bronzing" or burning a logo into the outside of the lid. Although not always oval in shape, they incorporated the central image or at least a tie-in to the general theme of the product. Unlike the wide spread interest in the larger outers, we know of no one who specializes in collecting these ovals, but it is always a good idea to add some of these ancillary pieces if you own the outer image.

BACK FLAPS

Less than a third of cigar makers ordered and used the back flap, since many felt it was not necessary. The main benefit was to show the retailer the brand name whenever the lid was not visible. This fact alone makes them much rarer than other trimmings.

1. *American Protectorate* *
2. *Bill Fold* *
3. *Queen Mary* *
4. *Julian Eltinge* *
5. *Quaker Girl* *
6. *O'Hara's Best* *

CAUTION LABELS

In 1868, after discovering that many small retailers were refilling empty boxes with cigars that had not been taxed, Congress passed a law that required the placement of a caution notice on each and every box. To avoid the expense of one more label, many cigar makers printed the warning directly on the bottom of the box. Makers with larger budgets ordered caution labels with artwork matching the other trimmings. Like back flaps, caution labels are quite limited in availability.

1. *Lucky Bill* *
2. *Supreme Court* **
3. *Flor de Rosas* *

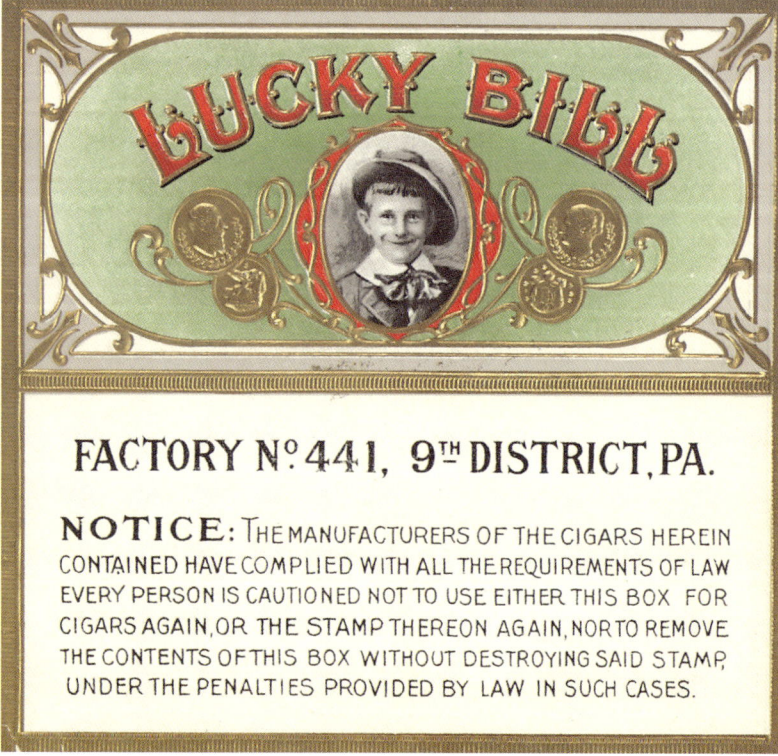

5.

6.

2.

3.

THE PACKAGE ART • *Trimmings*

NAIL TAGS

There are individuals in at least three countries (including the United States) who collect the small, but ornate nail tags almost exclusively. Easily displayed in a variety of album pages — from photos to baseball card size — they certainly occupy a unique niche in the collecting world. As with many of the other trimmings, nail tags usually display some part of the main theme.

1. *Bingo* * Since the inner logo was diamond-shaped, the maker carried it over to the nail tag.
2. *California Rose* * Typical scalloped border oval.
3. *Lincoln Park Bouquet* * Harris Litho letterpressed custom titles on their nail tags, as in this example.
4. *Our Guarantee* * This tag, featuring the elephant "Tusko," is die-cut like a notary seal.
5. *Tom Mix* * This nail tag simulates a sheriff's badge.
6. *Winner* * Unique horseshoe die-cut.
7. *Untitled* * Cowboy on horseback with rifle.
8. *Untitled* * Indian maid.
9. *Untitled* * Draped coat of arms.
10. *Untitled* * Unitas Brand used the same stone as the inner.
11. *Untitled* ** Minstrels dancing.

6. 5. 10.

CIGAR BOX EDGINGS

The primary purpose of cigar box edging was obviously decorative, but it also served to cover the muslin hinge that attached the lid. Edgings were usually ordered from the same lithographer who supplied the other trimmings, but only the larger, more successful cigar makers ordered custom-designed edging, since "stock" edgings were available at much lower cost.

1. *Flor Fina.* Stock edging, red and gold.
2. *Montana Sport.*
3. *High Sovereign.*

1.

Cigar Boxes

Cigar boxes were the first modern packages to seriously and competitively use a combination of labeling and package design to attract customers at the point of sale. No other product in history has been packaged and labeled in more different ways than the cigar. Nearly every sales and design gimmick, slogan, and guarantee used today was first used by cigar makers and retailers more than a century ago.

The cigar industry involves staggering numbers. Two hundred thousand cigar factories combined to sell ten billion boxes of cigars. To do that, more than 2,000,000 different combinations of boxes and label were tried. Today, afficionados of advertising and package design eagerly hunt pre-1960 boxes for their richness of variety. Cigar boxes are considered by many to be "the perfect package." Each box identifies the product, sells the product, protects the product, and displays the product. In addition they are easily stored, useful when empty, and recyclable as well. This chapter is intended as the briefest of introductions to this amazing package.

Readers who collect label art may be surprised to learn that less than 2% of the labels in their collection have ever been found on boxes. Many labels are known only on cigar boxes.

Modern cigar boxes began in the Civil War. Federal tax officials demanded that all cigars be packed in boxes

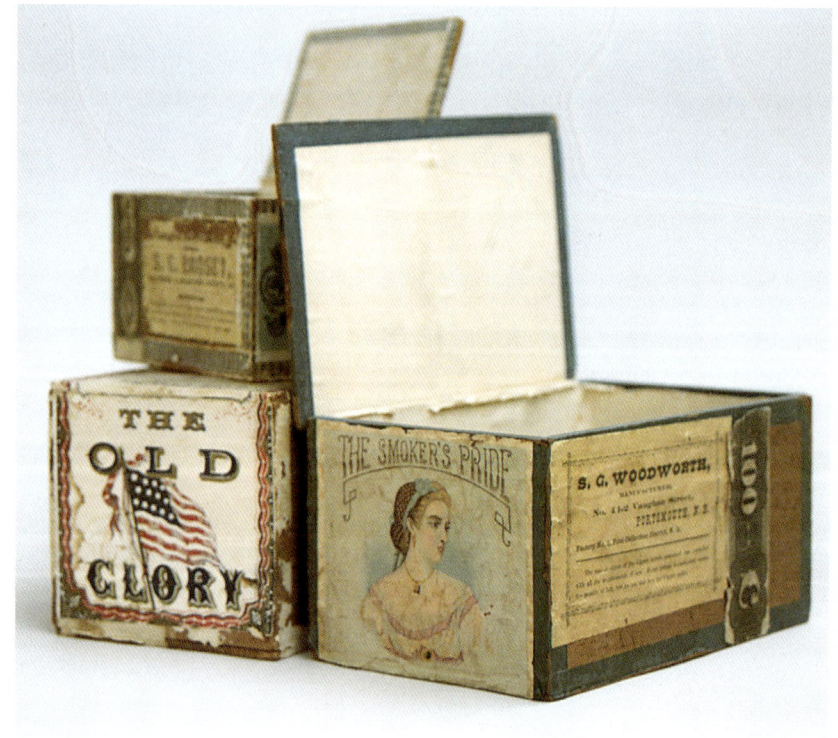

1. *The Old Glory*, trimmed wood 100/13, Utica, NY, 1866****
The Smokers Pride, trimmed wood 100/13, Portsmouth, NH, 1872*****
Champion, trimmed wood 25/5, Lancaster County, 1874**

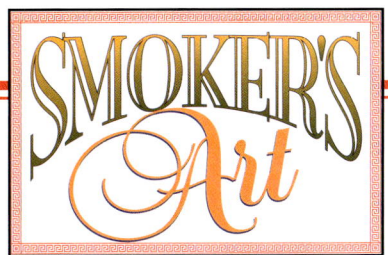

so they could be counted and taxed. The earliest U.S. boxes (1860's) were labeled only on one end because they were displayed closed on shelves, usually behind the proprietor. Brand names were simple. There was little competition. In most parts of America, a cigar was a cigar, and you pretty much took what you could get. Inside lids were almost always blank paper. (*See Figure 1.*)

At first, the outer label was the only place a cigar could be advertised. This Cuban looking outer label depicts a tobacco worker puffing away, happily endorsing the contents. The style, wording and company address duplicate that used by Cuban cigar makers since the 1840's. The inside label was not considered important by this cigarmaker, who filled it with plain lace on a pale

2. *El Plantador*, trimmed wood 100/13, Indiana, 1869 ****

background, omitting both his name and that of his product. *(See figure 2)*

In the early 1870's, demand for cigars increased. Thousands of small companies and a handful of giants competed. Most cigars were sold within a day's travel of where they were made. Cost cutting competition among cigarmen led to the use of molds and unskilled labor. This led to a flood of inferior cigars. Cigar counter showcases were developed to allow retailers to display boxes open so the cigars could be seen. That made the inside of the box lid visible and encouraged the use of brand names and graphics to catch a smoker's eye. Cigar makers, box makers,

3. *Defiance*, trimmed wood 50/13, Lancaster County, PA, 1876 ***

4. *Dew Drop,* trimmed wood 100/13, Maine, 1878 ***

label printers, wholesalers, retailers, even the smokers themselves got involved in box and label design.

Cigarmen were among the first retailers to use pretty girls to move product. This woman didn't have a name, but the top brand identified the contents as *Defiance* cigars. The very early outer label was modified to become an inner by flanking it with decoration. Outers used as inners, plain or decoratively flanked in some way, can be found on boxes as late as 1885, but are thought of as typical of the 1870's. A few larger brands, notably *Robt. Burns, Pippins,* and *Papoose,* kept their traditional 1870's style of label into the 1930's. *(See Figure 3)*

The artistic use of typefaces and borders is typical of 19th century broadsides. These wordy typeface-dominated labels were rarely used past 1885. This particular combination of label and trim results in an attractive, functional, well designed small box without using color or much ornamentatio *(see figure 4)*

The Golden Age of cigars lasted until the 1920's and 1930's when mechanization and cost-cutting forced four of every five

All Points, trimmed wood 50/13, Reading, PA, 1903
*** empty **** full

5. *Cabin Home*, log cabin 100/13, New York City, c1883 ****

factories to fold. But for fifty years, cigar factories were found in every state, with New York, Pennsylvania and Ohio the largest producers. When it came to selling all those cigars, there were no restrictions on what could be said on a cigar label or box. As long as manufacturers paid the Feds their taxes, the only requirement was that each box be identified as to the maker in small print on the bottom and a caution notice be applied telling makers and vendors they were not permitted to use the box for cigars again. Other than that, a box and label could depict, claim or imply anything. This freedom made for creative marketing that has never been equaled. A great deal of it would today be illegal or grounds for lawsuit.

Every year, nine of every ten cigars made were packed in standard nailed wood boxes trimmed with inner, outer, edging, and liner, accompanied by the Government's required caution notice. Some boxes added signature tags, distributor's stickers, top ovals, bands on the cigars, and various styles of flaps.

All Points provides a look at how a typical turn-of-the-century nailed wood box was trimmed. Note the revenue stamp that wraps completely around the box. This size stamp is found only on boxes before 1910.

Tax laws governing cigar boxes were strict, requiring cigars to be packed in rectangular wooden boxes of 25, 50, 100, 250 or 500 cigars. Boxes were

6. *Merry Christmas*, book 25/13, Western NY, c1906 **
Holiday Greetings, book 25/13, Wisconsin, c1905 **
Compliments of the Season, book 25/13, Iowa, c1911 **

7. *Hustler*, trimmed wood 12/6, Lancaster County, c1904 ***

not required to be trimmed (covered with labels). As a result, some cigarmakers cut costs by having their ad copy printed directly on the wood. The lid on this type box was typically attached with brass hinges, and the box frequently had a clasp. It was difficult to print complex pictures on wood, so ad copy was often a few simple words in a decorative border. The style was fairly popular until the 1920's and remained a special order item in boxmaker's catalogs into the 1950's.

In 1878, tax laws restricting the shape of boxes were loosened. Cigars could be sold in boxes made of any material made in any shape, as long as they held the required number of cigars and and allowed a tax stamp to be affixed. Within three years boxes appeared shaped like books, bottles, game boards, giant cigars, steamer trunks, drop front desks, cheese boxes, railroad cars, barrels, humidors, even tree trunks. One of the more popular with consumers was the log cabin, last used in the 1930's. At least a half dozen varieties of cabins exist, all rare. This Cabin

8. *Recruit*, cardboard slip 10, Pennsylvania, 1909 **

9. *Knaup's Diplomacy*, trimmed wood 50/13, New York City, 1898 **

Home is the most frequently seen, although less than 20 are known. Blue liner was seldom used after the mid 1880's.*(See figure 5)*

Book-shaped boxes became the best known specialty shape, popular every Christmas since the 1880's. More than two-thirds of the 100+ known varieties of books have holiday labels. *(See figure 6)*

Small cigar boxes appeared on the market in 1892. Cigarmakers told legislators they needed a smaller package for "salesmen's samples." What they really wanted was a smaller less expensive box to compete with the growing popularity of cigarettes sold in 5¢ and 10¢ packages. Congress permitted boxes of 12 and 13 cigars which could be sold for 25¢ or 50¢ after 1891. This size box was popular for about twenty years, although still legal and used until the 1960's. This box depicts the most frequently seen configuration of a box of 12. *(See figure 7)*.

Boxes of 10 or 20 small cigarette-size cigars were first permitted in 1897. They were packed the same way as most cigarettes, in cardboard slide packs, usually stiffened with a trading card insert. Prior to that time, small cigars were classified, labeled, and taxed as "cigarettes." *(See figure 8)*

10. *no name pretty girl*, celluloid 25/13, New York City, c1905 ***

11. *Toboggans*, tin 50/13, Binghamton, NY, c1896 ****
   Prize Winners, tin 25/8, Binghamton, NY, c1896 ****

In the early 1890's it became possible to screen photographs and add them to cigar labels. Box collectors call these usually limited production items "vanity labels" and some consider them among their most rare boxes. Vanity labels picture cigar makers, their children, pets, race horses, stores, buildings, boats, marching bands, sports teams, gun clubs, and anything else that would stand still long enough to be photographed. This is probably Mr. Knaup, but why he called his cigars Diplomacy remains a mystery. *(See figure 9)*

Celluloid became a popular material for jewelry and other manufactured items around the turn of the century, so it's no surprise it found its way to cigar boxes. *(See figure 10)*

The technology to print on tin was developed near the end of the 19th century. Wm. Vogel Tinware in Brooklyn, NY, became the first to mass produce decorated tin cigar boxes, primarily for cigar makers in Binghamton, NY. Vogel's six different sports theme boxes were an immediate hit with consumers then and prizes for collectors today. Finding one of each is very difficult. They were made for only a few years and this very early paint has frequently been damaged by weather, handling, and natural deterioration of the paint bond. *(See figure 11)*

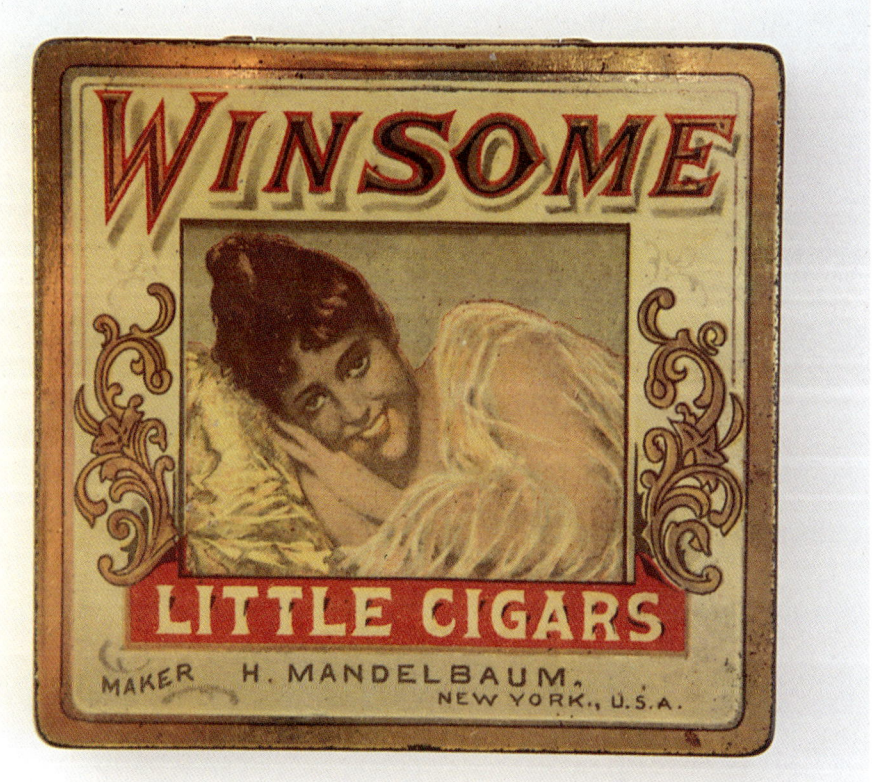

12. *Winsome*, flat ten, New York City, c1916 ***

13. *Tom Moore*, tin pocket pack, Detroit, MI 1926 **

Two popular forms of tin box (permitted after 1910) were the "pocket pack" of ten large cigars and the "flat ten" small cigar tin. Most popular in the 1920's but still used in the 1950's, they have been sought by collectors for more than two decades. There are barely 100 known collectible varieties cataloged at this time, but interesting items continue to turn up.(*See figures 12, 13)*

As the cigar industry depleted the world's cedar forests (making wood more expensive), tin cans became increasingly associated with cheap cigars. Some cans used paper labels as on boxes, but the cans prized by collectors had their advertising printed directly on the tin. Approximately 500 different cigar tins are known, most of them made in the 1920's. Tin slip top packages are still in use today. *(See figure 14)*

Cardboard rapidly replaced wood as the cigar box material of choice after World War II, but interesting cigar boxes are still being made in a variety of other materials.

14. *Pippins*, tin 25/up, Boston, c1916 ***   *50/50*, tin square 50/up w/display top, Pennsylvania, 1923 ***
Apache Trail, tin oval 50/up, Philadelphia, 1927 *****,   *War Eagle*, round tin 50/up, P.Lorillard, VA, c1925 ***
Careme, round tin 25/up, New York City, c1920 **

Cigar Bands

One of the benefits of a research project that entails poring through voluminous old publications and correspondence is discovering important facts that individuals of that period took for granted. One of the facts that jumped out at us immediately from a variety of sources was that the number one collectible in the United States during the period 1890–1915 was cigar bands! If that was truly the case (and we have no reason to doubt it), where are all those old collections today? Digging deeper, we discovered that less than 10% of the bands collected or saved ended up in collector's albums created especially for that purpose.

Just as the lady of the house kept cigar boxes to store jewelry and trinkets, the Novelty Company in Chicago sold découpage sets ($1.00 per set) with instruction sheets for applying the bands to the bottoms of clear glass ashtrays and dishes. Sometimes, using a nail tag, top oval — or in some cases, 4 x 4s — in the center, one could create a starburst of bands all the way out to the edge and then cover the bottom with felt.

Hundreds of examples of this découpage used to appear intermittently at flea markets and garage sales, ranging in size from five to twelve inches in diameter at $5 to $75 apiece. With the dramatic growth in desirability for anything tobacco-related, many of these are now realizing $75 to $125 each at auction.

On a much larger scale, some industrious and creative individuals — who didn't limit themselves to attaching the bands to ashtrays — began laminating them onto coffee tables, card tables, and large wall panels. Many of these pieces have ended up in museums and historical societies.

In an effort to sustain brand loyalty, quite a few cigar makers offered redemption prizes for turning in used bands. Long before anyone thought of offering rewards for turning in cereal box tops or logging air miles, turn-of-the-century cigar smokers could save up for anything, from a few free cigars to a fancy humidor. These programs alone were responsible for the redemption and subsequent destruction of millions of used bands.

8" BANDS FOR SIX CIGARS

Many collectible bands were produced by Gebrüber Weigang in Germany and sold by Heywood, Strasser & Voigt Litho, New York. A 1908 sample book lists small president bands at $1.25 per 1,000 net (25 to a set and sold in lots of no less than 500 of each of the 25 kinds), while the large president bands were $1.75 per 1,000 net (sold in similar lots).

So where are the collections that have survived? The lion's share of those that have surfaced is in European collections — primarily in Spain, Belgium, and Holland — where they were truly appreciated.

The competition for new varieties in Europe became so intense in the 1950s that European lithographers began printing "collector sets" of every possible subject matter, from animals and cars to royalty and flowers. Most American collectors were turned off by these photomechanical "contrived collectibles," but they were so cheap, some collectors couldn't pass them up.

Once in a while, when an "old" cigar band collection is offered for sale, you might find that a good percentage contains these European "sets," which dramatically lowers the total value and authenticity of the collection.

In building a collection, the prime consideration, as in most collectible fields, is condition. Advanced collectors use the following criteria for top quality: no creases, stains, or tears, and the full white tab must be intact and not cut off.

Many collectors used to be so particular that they wanted only portrait bands — those featuring presidents, actors, royalty, or animals. This restriction obviously leaves the collector with a comparatively small and limited collection. More importantly, as you can see in our examples, one really misses the boat on the broad diversity of themes and spectacular gilding available on many non-portrait bands. From a historical viewpoint, tens of thousands of different bands — representing just as many cigar makers — have survived, while the matching labels have not. This leaves the historian and tobacco collector with the only remaining physical record of that brand.

In our research, we found that two separate band-collecting groups existed. The International Cigar Band Society (1934–1951) were a grand group. They held fabulous conventions in New York City, toured factories, and even had a car (named "Queen I.C.B.S.") outfitted in colorful cigar bands and used to tour the country. Their newsletter showed their interest in historical facts. These people knew the history of each person or subject on the bands they owned.

The International Seal, Label and Cigar Band Society started in 1957 and lasted until 1994 or 1995. We joined in the 70s, and our membership number was 978, but the Society had over 1,000 members.

It seems that most of the major band collections we have purchased contained newsletters from one group or the other. (Joe Hruby, at 85 years of age, has collected bands for 70 years and joined the I.C.B.S. in 1940, as well as holding membership in the I.S.L.C.B.S.)

Nowadays, interest in bands is just beginning to reawaken, but there are still plenty of bargains available for you to build a viable collection for a reasonable investment. How to start? As with labels, certain pieces will determine the quality of your collection. Progressive proof books occasionally surface, as well as proof sheets or sample books. Presidential sets are highly coveted. So are playing cards, state seals, flags, alphabets, and fraternal organizations, to name but a few. In this section we will try to give an overview, but the choices are almost as diverse as the labels.

4" BANDS FOR TWO CIGARS

1. *Plucky Game.*
2. *Masterwork.*
3. *Seal Brand.*

The term "bunch bands" describes oversized bands that were used to hold two to twelve cigars sold in a bundle.

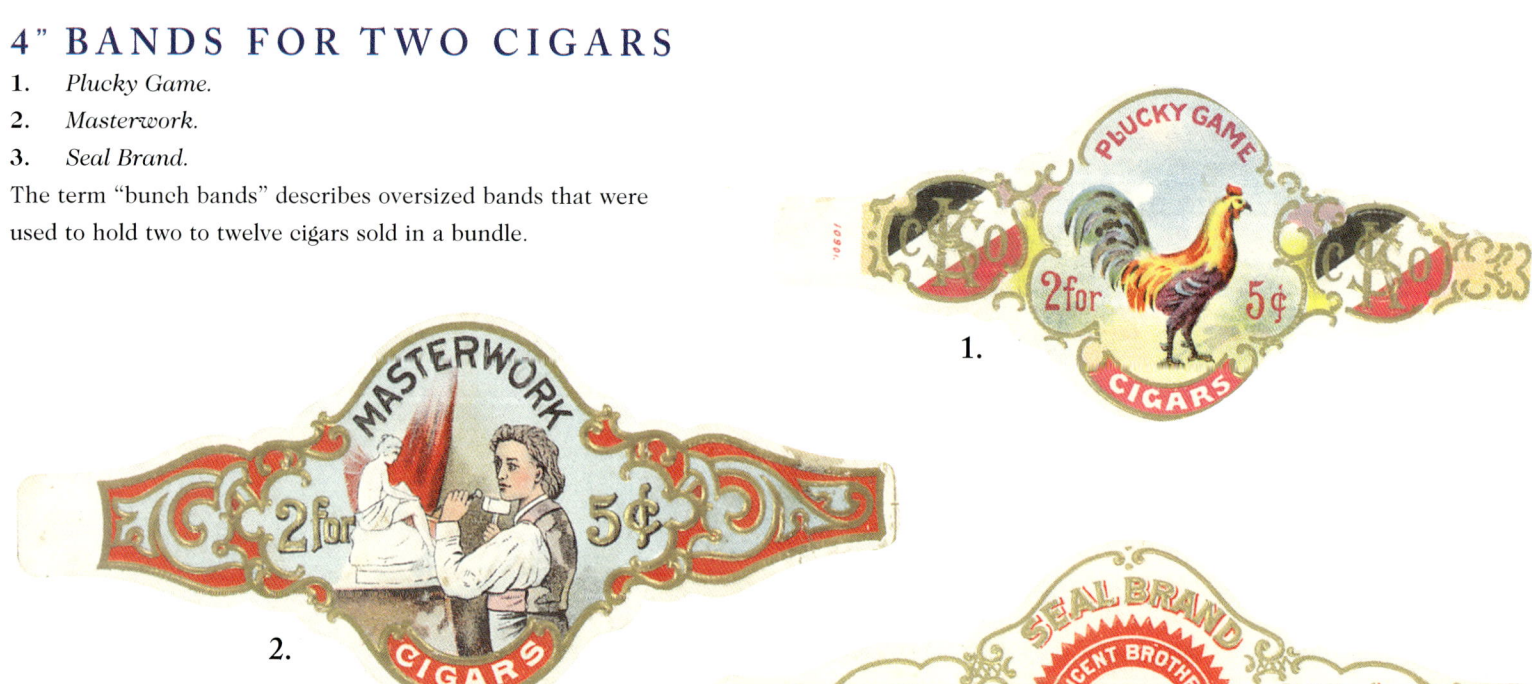

6" BANDS FOR THREE CIGARS

12" BANDS FOR TWELVE CIGARS

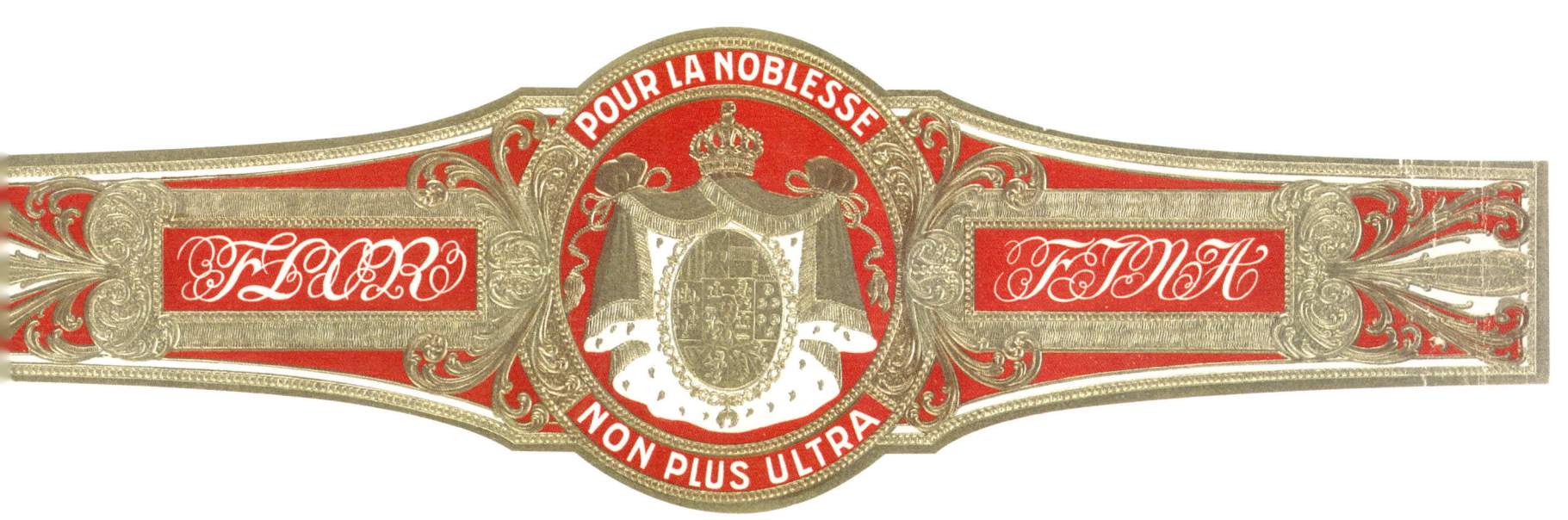

PRESIDENTS WITH VARIATIONS

8. Oval of U.S. Capitol sold with set of bands for découpaging to the bottoms of clear glass ashtrays and dishes.

9. *Benjamin Harrison.* PRINCEPS Belgium Cigar Manufact. Multicolored portrait, 25 bands, navy blue, circa 1901–1908..

10. *Grover Cleveland.* PRINCEPS Belgium Cigar Manufact. Multicolored portrait, 25 bands, navy blue, circa 1901-1908.

11. *William Taft.* PRINCEPS Belgium Cigar Manufact. Multicolored portrait, 26 bands, light blue, circa 1909. Rare variety with W. Taft.

12. *John Adams.* PRINCEPS Belgium Cigar Manufact. Portrait on golden background, 25 bands, circa 1900.

13. *Chester Arthur.* Embossed shield points outward. Embossing viewed best on reverse. 25 bands.

14. *James Monroe.* Shield points outward, shield not embossed. Non-embossing viewed best on reverse. 25 bands.

15. *James A. Garfield.* Shield inside and tabs with No. 4832/4856. Printed in Germany by Heinrich Duessen for Belgium Manufact. prior to 1925. 25 bands

16. *John Tyler.* Shield inside without numbers. Most found in United States. 25 bands.

17. *Benjamin Harrison.* Shield with towers or rooks outside. United States. 25 bands.

18. *George Washington.* Shield outside and laurel around image. United States. 25 bands.

24. Insert card of 25 presidents.

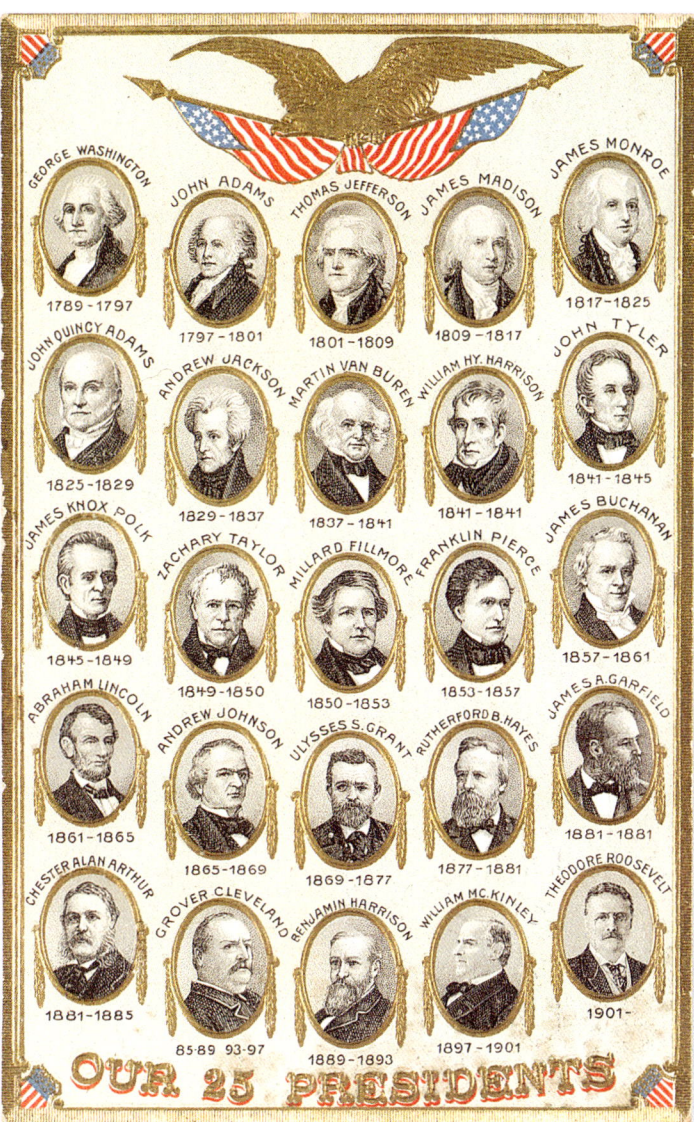

19. *Zachary Taylor.* Little laurel, portrait color on light blue background, gold eagles. United States. 25 bands.

20. *James A. Garfield.* Large laurel wreath around image, black & white portrait on gray background. United States. 25 bands.

21. *Wm. MacKinley.* Piccolina ("very little"). Printed 1902–1904. McKinley misspelled. 25 bands.

22. *Theodore Roosevelt.* Piccolina. Known varieties have tabs on right. Roosevelt, Adams, Taylor, Grant, Van Buren. United States. 25 bands.

23. *Zachary Taylor.* Piccolina. H. S.& V. on tabs. Printed 1902–1908. 25 bands.

THE PACKAGING ART • *Cigar Bands*

27.

28.

THE PACKAGING ART • *Cigar Bands*

FAMOUS & INFAMOUS PERSONALITIES

32. Adolph Hitler.
33. Benito Mussolini.
34. Ken Maynard, cowboy star.
35. Sir Thomas Lipton, sportsman, founder of Lipton Tea.
36. Eddie Edenburn, founder of Indy 500.
37. Julia Marlowe, actress.
38. Blanche Bates, actress.

34.

38.

32.

PUBLICITY BANDS

After perusing hundreds of variations, it is hard to believe how many different companies and organizations gave away or sold cigars in an effort to promote themselves.

MISCELLANEOUS GENRE

These examples are visual proof that the early collectors who limited themselves to collecting only portrait bands really missed the boat. The diversity of theme, along with the ornate gilding and embossing certainly justified saving them for posterity.

POST WORLD WAR II BANDS

These are photomechanically produced bands that were offered in sets of 12 to 24 pieces in Spain, Belgium, and Holland.

[

Caddy Label Art

When one first thinks of "smoker's art," there is no doubt that beautifully gilded and embossed stone litho cigar labels have certainly enjoyed the spotlight, but we must not overlook their distant cousins, the caddy labels produced between 1870 and 1915, for their unique place in both the art and smoker's worlds. Caddy labels were applied to the sides of 20- and 40-pound wooden shipping crates that contained tobacco "plugs," a highly compressed cake of tobacco blended and flavored for use in a pipe or for chewing.

Since both Richmond and Petersburg, Virginia were the primary centers of manufacturing and distribution, many of the labels that have survived bear the names of these cities.

Some manufacturer's names that appear most frequently on the labels include David Dunlop, Maclin-Zimmer-McGill, T. C. Williams, P. H. Mayo, William Cameron & Bros., Alex Cameron, and the British-American Tobacco Co. All these manufacturers were eventually taken over by the giant James B. Duke conglomerate, the American Tobacco Co.

As with cigar labels, printers also produced a variety of "stock" labels, which had blank openings for the names and cities of the smaller manufacturers who could not afford a custom label. As in any collectible field, some of these obscure brands are highly prized.

The lion's share of caddy labels was produced by A. Hoen & Company, which was located in the plug makers' back yard, Richmond, Virginia.

A few of the more prominent litho firms of the period also produced caddy labels. You might recognize the following names: Calvert Litho in Detroit, Heppenheimer & Maurer, Kaufman and Strauss of New York, and Isaac Freidenwald Litho of Baltimore, Maryland. Images produced by these companies are highly coveted, not only for their art, but also their rarity.

If the artwork used on caddy labels appears to appeal to Anglophiles and seafarers, it was by no mistake. Over 80% of the plug-filled caddies went directly from the factories to the docks, where they were loaded for shipment to Australia, New Zealand, and Great Britain. Since the ultimate consumers in many cases were hard-working seamen, whalers, New Zealand stockmen, and Australian prospectors, this motivated lithographic artists

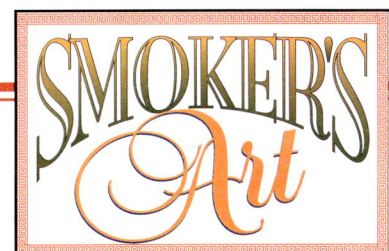

3.

to produce romantic themes of British Imperial history, adventure, and voluptuous maidens.

It is highly unlikely that any tangible record of this outstanding lithographic artwork would have survived, if it were not for the efforts of individuals like tobacco historian Bill Hatcher and Hilliard, Florida antique dealer, Frank Speal. Bill was one of the very first individuals to set eyes on these caddy labels and he realized their importance while helping the American Tobacco Co. consolidate some of their warehouses. Frank Speal's trained eye for high-quality art motivated him to beat the bushes of Richmond and Petersburg for months on end and even run ads in local papers. His efforts were eventually rewarded, and soon he had the largest inventory of any dealer in the United States.

A word of caution: as awareness and demand for these unique art forms has grown, it has also spawned a group of unethical sub-creatures who realize that today's color copiers can easily reproduce the caddy label's crayon style of artwork. Obviously, they cannot duplicate the paper, so in many cases they put them into frames. This does not mean that you should avoid buying framed pieces, but you should demand that the seller provide you with certified provenance as to its authenticity.

Fortunately, the little-known National Collectibles Act, enacted by Congress in the mid 1980s, provides severe punishment for anyone misrepresenting the age or authenticity of a collectible.

You will find most labels are of three approximate sizes: 7 x 14, 10 x 10, and 13 x 13.

1. *Banjo* **** A familiar image used on many products featuring Black subjects enjoying themselves. Unfortunately, this label has been reproduced and sold in frames at flea markets on the East Coast. Litho A. Hoen, Richmond, Va.
2. *Courage* *** This brand immortalized Lieutenants Melville and Coghill for attempting to save the Union Jack during the Zulu Wars. Litho A. Hoen, Richmond, Va.
3. *Harlequin* ** Strange theatrical theme used to market plug tobacco. Litho A. Hoen, Richmond, Va.(see page 229)
4. *The Celebrated Pipe Tobacco* **** Scarce label featuring a pipe. Isaac Friedenwald Litho.
5. *The Old Sport* ** Victorian artists loved to show animals. Litho Liebler & Maass, N.Y.

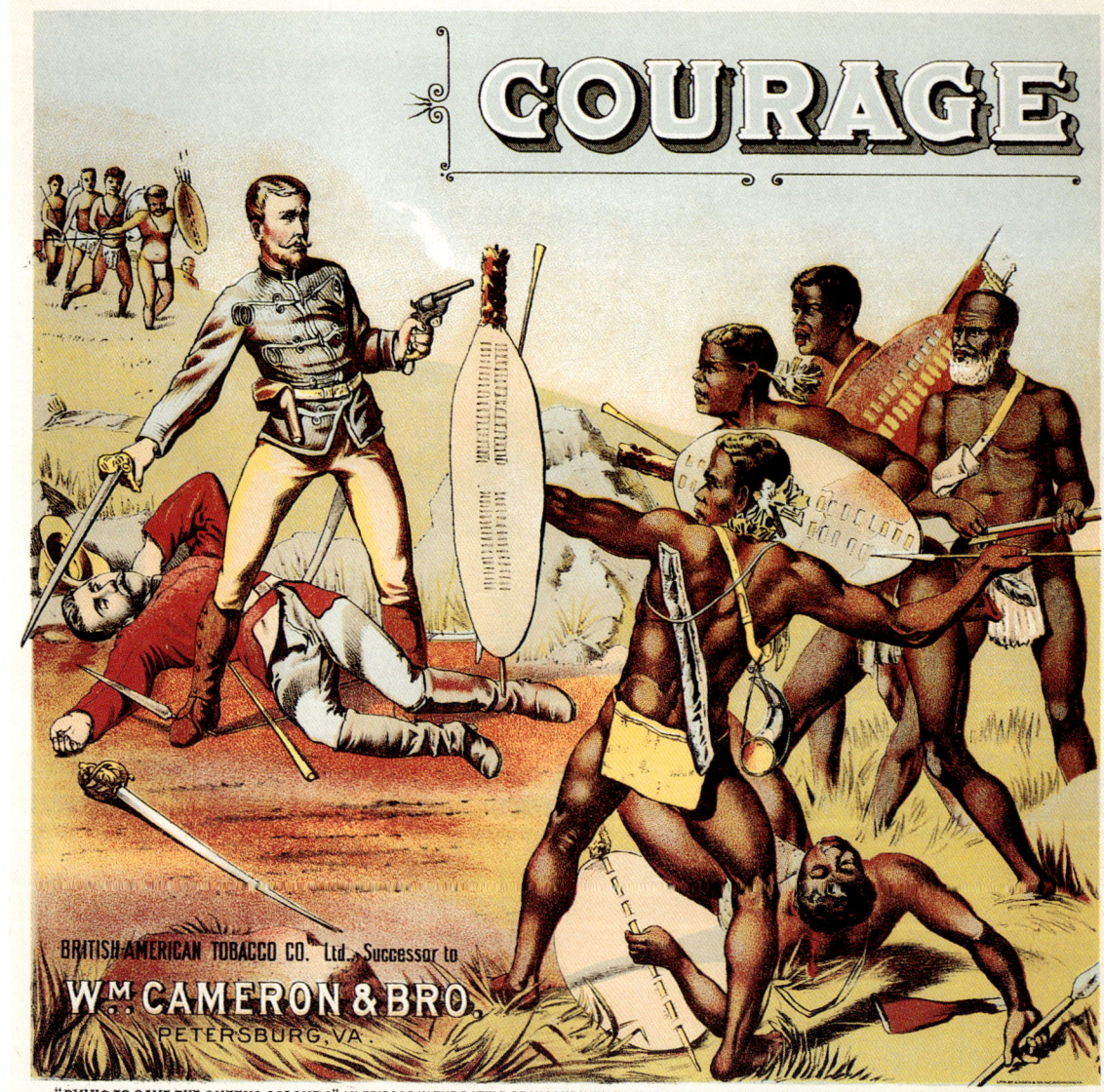

4.

6. *Octoroon* *** The term used for anyone who was one-eighth Black, also known as "high yellow." Litho A. Hoen, Richmond, Va.

7. *The Queen* **** Queen Victoria ruled the most powerful nation in the world when this label was produced in 1882. The Knapp Co. Litho, New York.

8. *Tough Chew* ***** Imaginative and humorous artwork by Calvert Litho, using children and animals.

9. *The Derby* *** Great 19th-century racing scene.
10. *Victory* ** These 1870s artists weren't afraid to show a little blood. A. Hoen and Company, Richmond, Va.
11. *Wealth of Nations* **** Edward VII appeared on many cigar bands and labels, but the caddy label artist had a much larger format to work with.

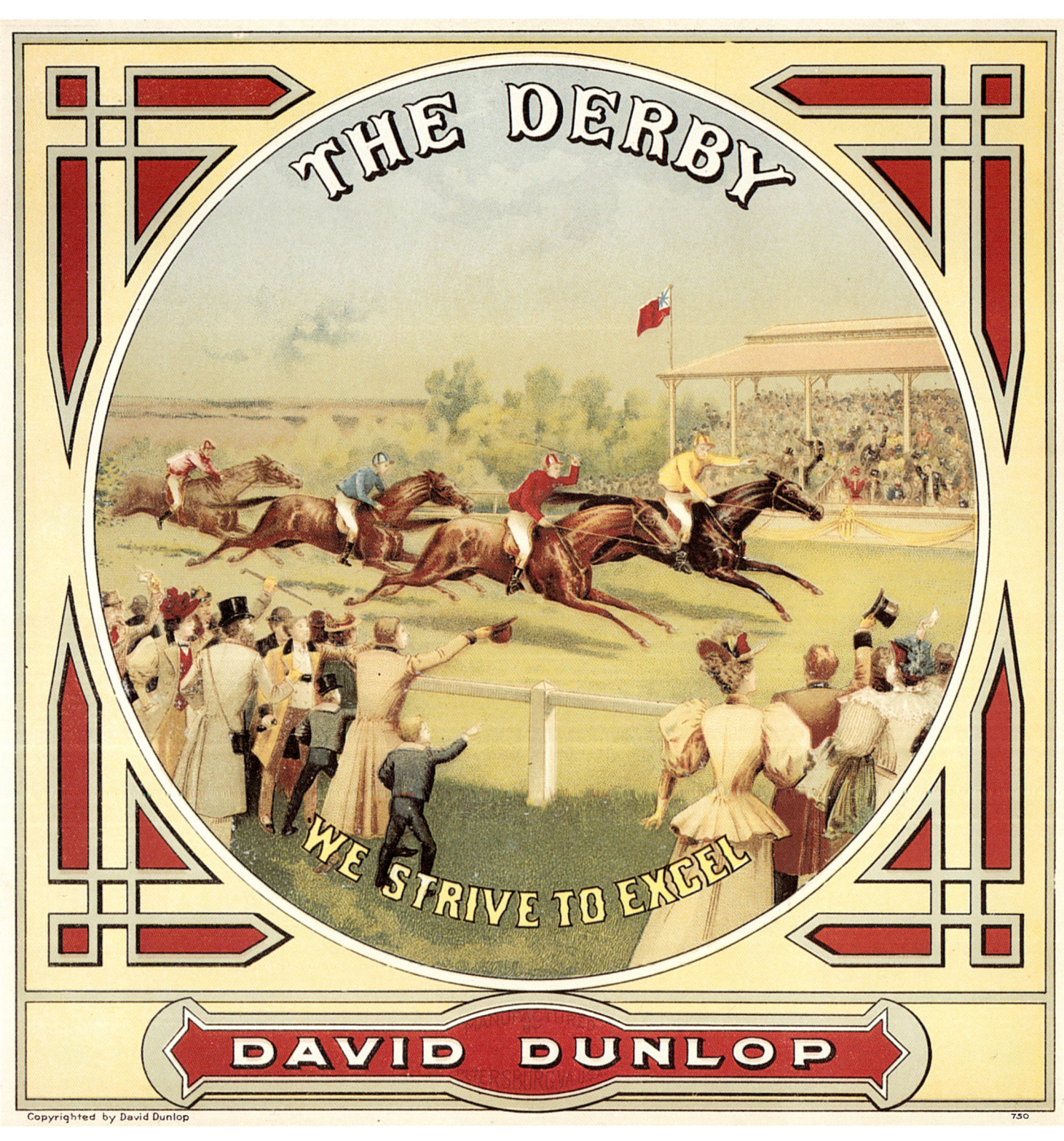

9.

10.

11.

12. *Welcome Nugget* ** The world-renowned discovery of a gigantic 2,217-ounce gold nugget in Australia was immortalized on a caddy label.
13. *Southdown* * Image of sheep appealing to New Zealanders or very lonely sailors. Maclin-Zimmer-McGill Co.

13.

14 *La Plata* ** Striking use of only three colors featuring Centennial Expo. Litho A. Hoen, Richmond, Va

15 *The Rivals* ***1875 image picturing fife at a British outpost. The "Only Single Lady at the Station" Litho A. Hoen, Richmond, Va.

15.

14.

16 *Crusader* ** The Crusades were still a popular subject in the 1800s. Watson & McGill, Petersburg, Va.
17 *"Jolly Boy"* ** British cavalryman lighting his pipe. Litho Heppenheimer & Maurer, NY.
18 *Untitled,* *** Loyal girlfriend waiting on shore for her lover. Maclin-Zimmer-McGill Co. Petersburg, Va.
19 *Untitled,* ** Draped girl and doves. Litho A. Hoen, Richmond, Va.

19.

17.

18.

16.

Cigarette Pack Art

When you think of high-quality, superbly embossed and gilded labels, you may imagine that cigarette pack and smoking tobacco labels are not the first images that come to mind. Think again! Because of the fierce competition among cigar makers during the gilded age, lithographers were virtually given a blank check to produce the finest and most ornate images possible. The fledgling American makers of cigarette and smoking tobacco (plain, roll-your-own, etc.) became the first beneficiaries of litho technology and took immediate advantage of it.

It is believed that cigarette smoking evolved from pipe smoking and not cigar smoking. The "factory-blended" cigarette came about in reponse to people using blended pipe tobaccos for "roll-your-owns."

In spite of spectacular packaging, it still took decades before these types of smoking tobacco mixtures caught on.

Cigarette smoking took hold in Britain in 1856, when troops returned from the Crimean War with their "Turkish trophies" of war. By 1870, New York tobacconists began hiring European cigarette rollers who produced fragrant and aromatic Turkish and Russian blends that appealed to both men and women. Virginia was soon importing rollers from New York to keep up with the demand.

The first cigarette-making machine was built in 1883, but it was thirty years before it was finally used by a major national cigarette company. Before the machine, the best that hand rollers could do was four to five cigarettes per minute.

The new fad caused one New York observer to comment: "Some of the ladies of this refined and fashion-forming city are aping the silly ways of some pseudo-accomplished foreigners by smoking tobacco through a weaker and more feminine article called the cigarette." Regardless of such criticisms, cigarettes and blended tobacco were here to stay.

In the seminal stages of marketing cigarettes, the labels were affixed to cardboard boxes that either slid

1.

open like a matchbox or had a lid that opened like a cigar box. Along with the introduction of more automated methods of producing cigarettes came the introduction of the "soft pack," still in use today, which cut packaging costs dramatically. Unfortunately, it also virtually eliminated the heavily gilded and embossed labels used on the earlier box formats.

Unlike other members of the antique label family, no significant quantities or bundles of early cigarette labels have been discovered. Most of the ones that have surfaced were in proof or sample form from lithographers' reference files. A number of dedicated collectors worldwide collect the complete packs and boxes and have built some pretty spectacular collections. Unfortunately, the early embossed images usually represent a very small percentage of their collections.

Nevertheless, we are thankful for collectors! Some of the finest artworks in the world are in private collections, and owned by people who truly appreciate their history.

1. *Omar.* American Tobacco Company. (see page 263)
2. *Helmar.* Turkish cigarettes.
3. *Ramleh.* Turkish cigarettes.
4. *Snow Shoe Smoking or Chewing Tobacco.* Scotten-Dillon Co., Detroit, Michigan.
5. *Four Aces Smoking.* The Friedenwald Co., Baltimore, Maryland.
6. *Jack Rabbit Smoking Tobacco.* The Friedenwald Co., Baltimore, Maryland.

2.

3.

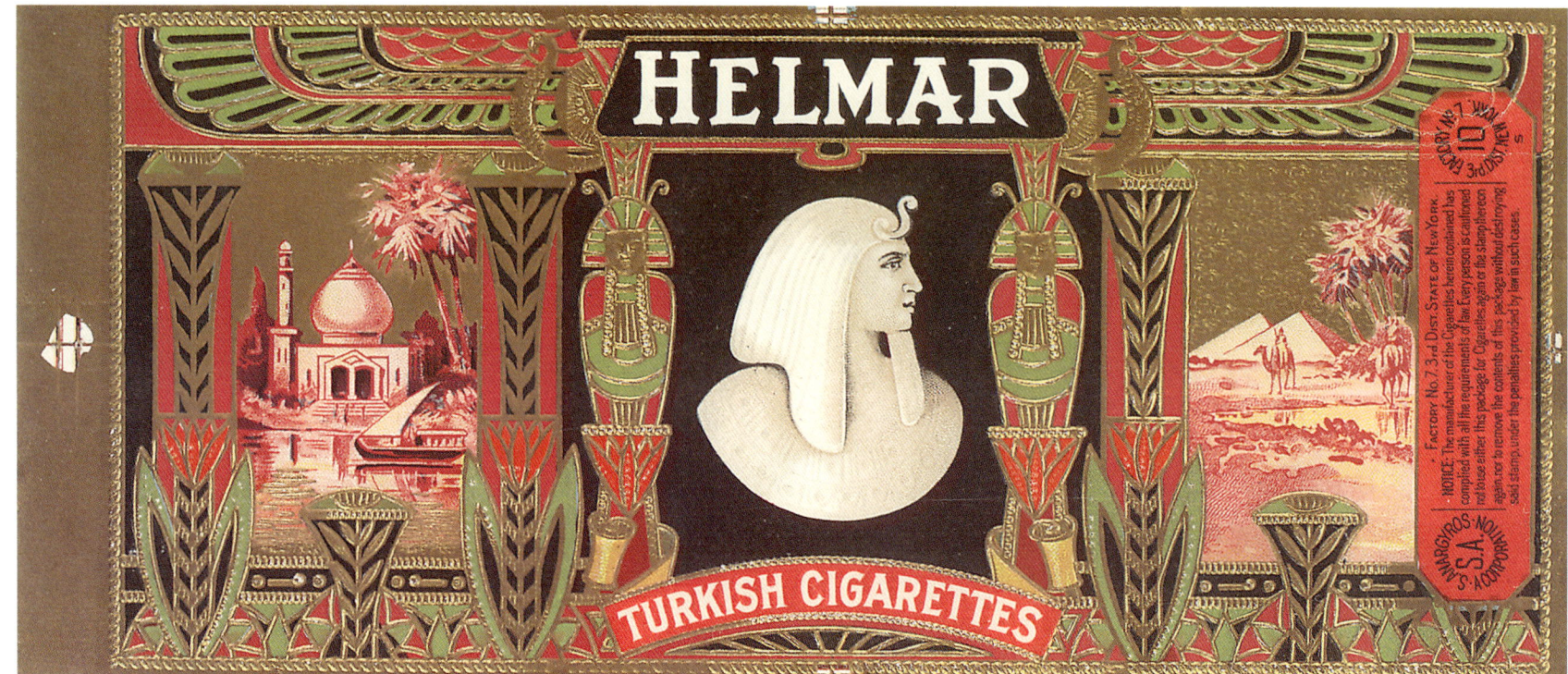

4.

Snow Shoe

6.

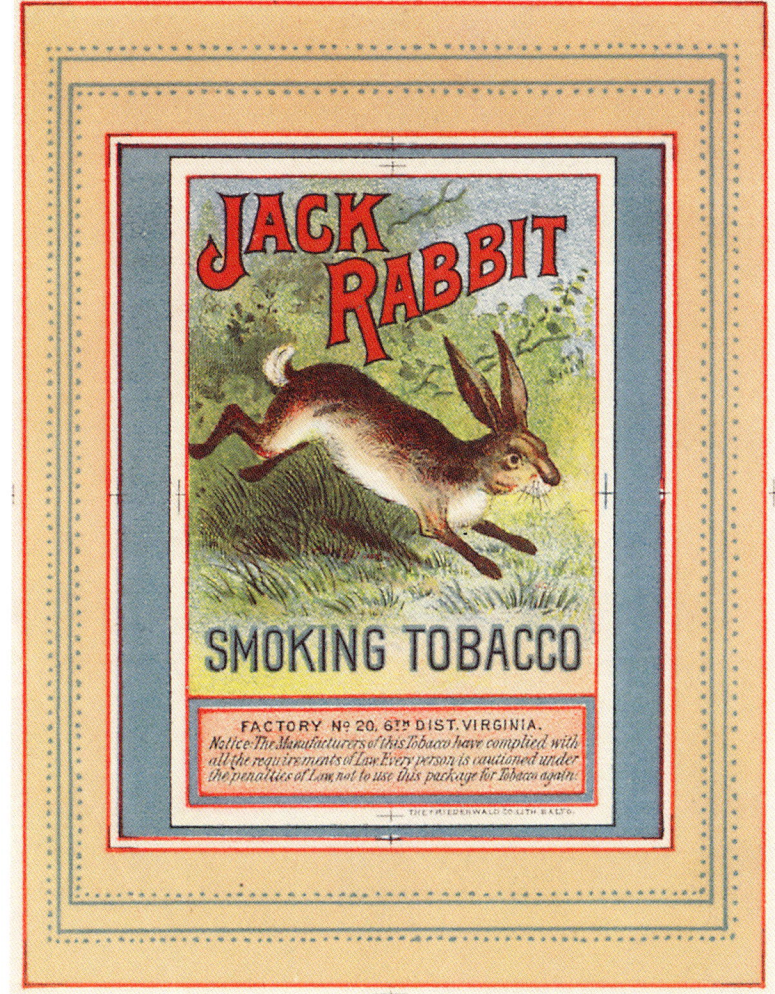

5.

7. *El Principe de Gales.* Havana cigarettes.
8. *Beauty Joseph.* Egyptian Cigarettes.
9. *Mogul.* Egyptian Cigarettes.
10. *Salim Milan.* Egyptian Cigarettes.
11. *Pirate Cigarettes.*
12. *Menthorets.* Consolidated Litho, 1928.
13. *New York Cigarettes.* British-American Tobacco Co.

7.

8.

9.

10.

11.
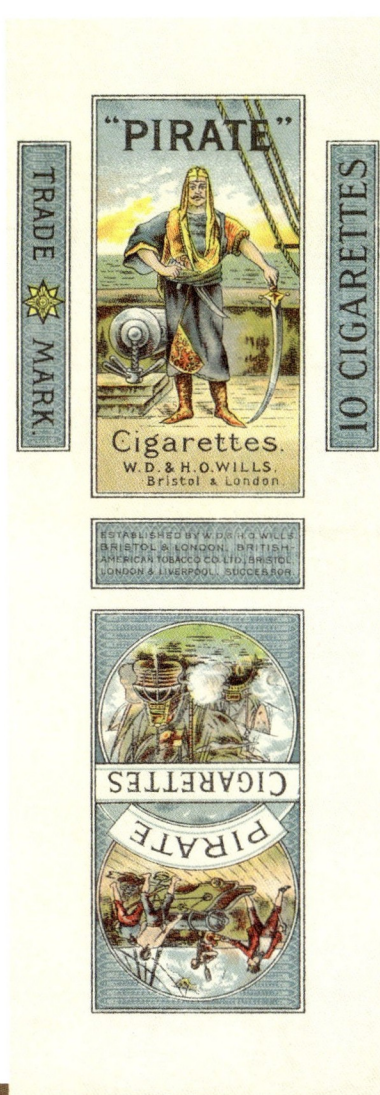

13.

12.

Resource Information

Past Publications and Other Resource Information

In an effort to broaden your library of information concerning these fascinating art works and their growth in popularity, here is a listing of some past publications that had feature stories about Smoker's Art and a few sources you can contact directly.

FORTUNE MAGAZINE, February 1933
    At the height of the depression, cigar bands were probably the most popular collectible over coins and stamps primarily due to cost and availability. This issue contained an original stone litho insert of bands produced from the original stones owned by Consolidated Litho. Featured in the montage of bands is the coveted Coca-Cola band.

FORTUNE MAGAZINE, March 1933
    One of the earliest "awareness" stories recognizing cigar labels as superior art works. This issue has a full four page spread of actual stone litho prints.

ESQUIRE MAGAZINE, February 1949
    Two page story in color showing dozens of rare and coveted labels.

CIGAR LABEL A-R-T, A. D. Faber, Century House, 1949.

VITOLFILIA, Alfredo Garcia Paladini, Madrid, 1952
    386 pages on the hobby of band collecting.

EROS, Summer 1962 (Hardbound)
    This hardbound issue is a unique collectible in itself since only four issues were published by Ralph Ginzburg. Includes six full color pages of exotic women on cigar labels.

COLLECTORS NEWS, September 1977
    Cover story with colored pictures of rare cigar labels.

POTENTIALS IN MARKETING MAGAZINE, September 1978
    Cigar art featured on cover--full color.

AMERICAN HERITAGE, December 1978

TIME-LIFE ENCYCLOPEDIA OF COLLECTIBLES, Vol. 4, 1978

HANDBOOK OF AMERICAN CIGAR BOXES, Tony Hyman 1979
    A "must read" for those interested in collecting cigar boxes. 176 pp; 200+ illustrations.

CLEVELAND PRESS, March 16, 1979
    Full page story, first page of Connoisseur Section.

CLEVELAND PLAIN DEALER, SUNDAY MAGAZINE, April 1, 1979
    Six page story in full color devoted to cigar art.

WALL STREET JOURNAL, September 7, 1979
    Front page feature story on the dramatic growth of cigar labels on the collectibles market, 3/4 page story plus graphics.

MILWAUKEE JOURNAL, SUNDAY MAGAZINE, June 29, 1980
    Five page story in full color.

CINCINNATI ENQUIRER, June 27, 1981
    Front page story.

SMOKESHOP NEWS MAGAZINE, June 1982

GREENSBURG TRIBUNE REVIEW (PA), September 26, 1982

WESTERN RESERVE MAGAZINE, November-December, 1982

JUNIOR ACHIEVEMENT MAGAZINE, April 1983
    Story with pictures about youth earning thousands of dollars framing and selling cigar art.

MEDINA COUNTY GAZETTE (OH), January 2, 1985
    Two page story.

ELYRIA CHRONICAL TELEGRAM (OH), Sunday, February 10, 1985
    Cover story in full color.

MICHIANA / SOUTH BEND TRIBUNE, June 16, 1985
    Five page color story in Sunday Magazine.
THE DETROIT NEWS, August 24, 1985
    Front page story.
AKRON BEACON JOURNAL (OH), August 25, 1985
    Six page story in full color in Sunday Magazine.
TIFFIN ADVERTISER-TRIBUNE (OH), October 23, 1986
TOLEDO BLADE (OH), July 19-25, 1987
    Four page story in full color in Sunday Magazine.
COLLECTORS' SHOWCASE, July/August 1987 Vol. 6 No. 6
    One article (8 pages) titled Cigar Boxes by Tony Hyman. The second article is America's Cup Cigar Labels by Eva Ditler. Both are in full color.
A VICTORIAN SCRAPBOOK, Cynthia Hart, John Grossman and Priscilla Dunhill, Workman Publishing, 1989, 152 pp.
    Portraying Victorian life and times, using great cigar labels throughout.
THE ART OF THE CIGAR LABEL, Joe Davidson. Wellfleet Press, 1989, 252 pp. Beautifully produced collectibles book that ended up as a best seller.
THE WORLD OF SMOKING AND TOBACCO AT AUCTION, Tony Hyman, 1989
    A wonderful catalog in color and black & white, with descriptions.
PARLOR CATS, Cynthia Hart, John Grossman and Josephine Banks, Workman Publishing, 1991, 92 pp.
    Portraying Victorian cats, using antique ephemera, including cigar art.
OFFICIAL PRICE GUIDE OF CIGAR LABEL ART, The American Antique Graphics Society, 1993.
    As with most price guides, the prices quoted were obsolete by the time the ink was dry, but it does contain other
    important information.   First time any list over 5,000 images was published.
CIGAR AFICIONADO MAGAZINE Summer 1994
    "The Art of Cigar Boxes" five page delightful article by Tony Hyman.
CIGAR AFICIONADO MAGAZINE Winter 1994
    "The Band" five page article about cigar bands by Tony Hyman
SMOKE MAGAZINE, Premier Issue, Vol. 1, Issue 1, Holiday Season, 1995
    "Investing in History" four page article and labels by Joe Davidson.
THE TOBACCO INDUSTRY IN CUBA AND FLORIDA, Narciso G. Menocal, 1996.
CIGAR AFICIONADO'S WORLD OF CIGARS, Edited by Marvin Shanken, Running Press, 1996
    136 pp. Beautiful recaps from the magazine. Tony Hyman's two previous articles are included.

Calendars

JOHN GROSSMAN'S VICTORIAN CHARMS, Day Dream Publishing,1996, 1997, 1998
CIGAR LABEL ART, Cedco Publishing, from the collection of The Gifted Line, 1998
VINTAGE CIGAR LABELS, Hallmark Cards, from the Joe Davidson Collection, 1998

Other Resources

TONY HYMAN
    This man has collected cigar boxes since 1952, writes a monthly Tobacciana Q & A column in the Antique Trader and has a
     syndicated weekly radio show. Visit Tobacciana.com or write to him at P. O. Box 3000, Shell Beach, CA   93449
CIGAR LABEL COLLECTORS INTERNATIONAL
    The oldest and largest cigar label collectors organization, beginning Winter of 1993. Provides factual information concerning upcoming
    auctions, price trends, new discoveries and articles by credentialed experts in their quarterly publication, The Stone Press. Ed and
    Laura Harrison, editor. Contact C. L. C. I. at P. O. Box 66, Sharon Center, Ohio 44274 Yearly dues and subscription $10.00.
AMERICAN ANTIQUE GRAPHICS SOCIETY
    Official appraiser for museum and university collections of 100 to 700 year old graphic art works. Published the Official Price Guide
     of Cigar Label Art in 1993 and has conducted semi annual consignment auctions (Spring & Fall) of Tobacco related artifacts
     and labels since 1983. Contact A. A. G. S. at P. O. Box 924, Medina, Ohio 44258 or phone (330) 723-7172.

Internet Warning:

Since the Internet is still in its seminal stage of experimentation in a variety of areas, we advise a word of caution for anyone who might want to use this medium for either information or resources.

We see great potential in the future for this medium, but at present, misinformation and potential scams abound on the net. So let the buyer beware.

Most importantly, never, never send anyone a high resolution copy, photograph or the original of anything in your collection, regardless of what they tell you they want it for. Chances are, you'll soon see your priceless image begin to appear in all kinds of areas and they never had to pay you a licensing fee, let alone share the profit with you!

Museum Collections

With all the new museums cropping up, be they public or private, there is no doubt in our minds that a museum dedicated to cigar labels with their broad spectrum of themes and quality of art is long overdue.

The Gundlach Group, owners of the spectacular Klingenberg Litho archives in Germany is planning one dedicated to Stone Lithography with a possible site in Bielefeld, Germany, but that is down the road. Until then, or, if you don't want to travel to Germany, there are a number of museums, universities and libraries that own cigar label collections.

As we are sure you are aware, almost 90% of any museum's collections are in the "back room" so you must always inquire of the curators if they have a collection of cigar art. If they do, they will usually give you a private showing with some advance notice on you part. Surprisingly enough, we have never visited a museum that did not have some cigar memorabilia in their collections, from the Chicago Historical Society with Lincoln labels to the Custer Museum in Monroe, Michigan whose hero appeared on a few early cigar labels. Public Libraries should not be overlooked either, since they also accept a variety of donations. In fact, the Cleveland Public Library has an outstanding cigar band collection which we would have never been aware of if it hadn't come up in conversation during one of our research missions.

So ask your local museum, historical society public library or university if they have any ephemeral collections containing cigar labels and we're sure you'll probably be surprised. They might even want to deaccession it to you, or, on the other hand, you could always donate some of your duplicates!

Here are a few institutions that have cigar art in their archives as of this writing:
1. Smithsonian Institute, Washington, DC
2. Museum of American Folk Art, New York, NY
3. University of South Florida, Tampa, FL
4. Art Gallery of Windsor, Windsor, Ontario, Canada

The Authors

Just as tobacco was elevated from the Caribbean jungles to the royal courts of Europe, the Davidsons will be best remembered for elevating tobacco label art from the concrete jungle to some of the most prestigious galleries and museums in the world.

Having generated millions of dollars in the consumer products world in the early 1970s, one might assume that they would apply the same success formula to their discoveries in the antique graphics world, including tobacco-related artworks. However, the major difference in this new field is the Davidsons' love and respect for these unique artifacts, whose historical and esthetic appeal cannot be matched by the consumer products of today.

Considering the fact that they first introduced cigar label art in conjunction with their broad line of 100- to 700-year-old antique graphics in 1978, tobacco art was obviously not an overnight success.

Undaunted by the negativism emanating from anti-tobacco factions and paper dealers who did not understand or appreciate chromolithography, the Davidsons finally developed a large and appreciative audience at the fine art gallery and executive gift level.

Encouraged and elated by the response at these levels, the Davidsons began to donate many rare and important artworks to institutions that would appreciate them, including the Smithsonian, The Western Reserve Historical Society, Detroit Institute of Art, Kent State University, and the Henry Ford Museum — all of whom turn down more offerings than they accept.

The Davidsons are kindred spirits with all dedicated collectors, and regardless of what fate holds for the world of tobacco art collecting, they have the satisfaction of knowing that they treated this hobby with the respect it deserves.

Index

AMERICAN COLORTYPE, 20, 21
AMERICAN LABEL, 21
AMERICAN LITHO, 18, 21, 30
AMERICAN TOBACCO CO., 228, 229
animals, 158–69
Art of the Cigar Label, The, 24, 26, 27
AUTOKRAFT BOX CO., 19

back flaps, 204–5
"banding," 179, 200
Bering, Vitus, 118
BRITISH-AMERICAN TOBACCO CO., 228
"bronzing," 202
"Buckeye" factories, 52, 74
"bunch bands," 216

CALVERT LITHO, 19, 21, 34, 228
CAMERON & BROS., WILLIAM, 228
cans. *See* tins
caution labels, 204–5, 209
CENTRAL LITHO, 16, 21
CHICAGO BOX CO., 21
chromolithography, 13
Churchill, Winston, 117, 120
cigarette-making machine, 242
cigarette smoking, origin, 242
cigars
    bands, 216–217

boxes, 178, 179, 200, 202, 208-16
    See also trimmings
consumption, 11
hand-rolled, 74
tins, 214–15
Civil War, 11, 208
COLE LITHO, 21
collecting, 23, 27, 217
"collector sets," 217
color bars, 31, 34
Columbus, Christopher, 10, 80, 120, 186
Concerning the Collection of Cigarbox Marks, 84
CONSOLIDATED LITHO, 18, 19, 20, 21
crayon lithography, 12
Curzon, Lord & Lady, 126, 134, 138

Davidson, Joe, 84
Day, Benjamin, 13
découpage, 216
Drew, John, 32

edgings, 207
embossing, 104
FIVE-CENT CIGAR CO., 117
"flat ten," 212
foxing, 25, 27
France

early lithography, 13
early tobacco use, 11
Franco, Generalissimo, 128
FRIEDENWALD, ISAAC, 21, 228

German lithographers, 20, 104
gold-leaf embossing, 104
grading system, 25–26
Grant, Ulysses S., 11, 120
Grossman, John, 25
GUNDLACH GROUP, 16

hand-rolled cigars, 74
hand stippling, 14, 28, 34
Hatcher, Bill, 229
HEPPENHEIMER & MAURER, 20, 21, 228
HEYWOOD, STRASSER & VOIGT, 21, 217
HOEN & CO., 21, 228
HOKLAS & SONS, 21
HOWELL, F. M., 21
Hruby, Joe, 218
Hyman, Tony, 84

International Cigar Band Society (I.C.B.S.), 218
International Seal, Label and Cigar Band Society (I.S.L.C.B.S.), 218

"junk packs," 178

Kane, Raymond P., 18, 19, 20
KAUFMAN-PASBACH-VOICE, 21
keyline drawing, 31
KLINGENBERG LITHO, 16, 17, 21, 23, 84, 104
KRUEGER & BRAUN, 20, 21

labels
    caddy, 228–41
    caution, 204–5, 209
    grading system, 25
    inner, 179
    outer, 179–201
    textual, 170–77
    value ranges, 26
Lincoln, Abraham, 72, 126
lithography
    chromolithography, 13
    crayon, 12
    embossing,
    German influence, 20, 104
    hand stippling, 14
    notable lithographers, 21
    photomechanical, 15
    planographic, 12
    rotary press, 15
    screen process, 14
    stone, 12–14

metal printing plates, 14–15
MOEHLE LITHO, 20, 21

nail tags, 178, 206–7

National Collectibles Act, 229

outer labels, 179–201
outer ovals, 202–3

photomechanical printing, 15
planographic printing process, 12
"plugs," 228
"pocket pack," 214

Quimby, Harriet, 134, 146

rarity, 24, 27, 34
rating system, 26
Revenue Act (1865), 200
Revolutionary War, 11
"roll-your-own," 242
rotary press, 15

SACKETT & WILHELMS, 21
sample books, 40–41
Schlegel, George, III, 17, 20
SCHLEGEL LITHO, 17, 20, 21, 34, 134
SCHÖTT, HERMANN, 21, 84, 104
Schott, Marge, 16
Schubert, Bernhard & Bina von, 16, 17, 20
SCHUMACHER & ETTLINGER, 20, 21
SCHWENCKE & PFITZMAYER, 21
SCHWENCKE, O. L., 20, 21
screen process, 14
Senefelder, Aloys, 12, 13
Smithson, James, 117
Spanish (and early tobacco use), 10

Speal, Frank, 229
"stock" labels, 52, 228
stone lithography, 12–14

tins, cigar, 214–115
tobacco
    consumption, 11
    introduction of, 10–11
    Puritan laws, 11
    Revolutionary War and, 11
trimmings
    back flaps, 204–5
    caution labels, 204–5
    edgings, 207
    nail tags, 178, 206–7
    outer labels, 179–201
    outer ovals, 202–3
    inners, 179

value ranges, 26, 31, 34
Vandeuren, Louis, 218
vanity labels, 212

wars
    Civil, 11, 208
    Crimean, 242
    Revolutionary, 11
    World War I, 84
    World War II, 22
    Zulu, 230
Washington, George, 11, 62, 194
West, Benjamin, 13
Wilhelm II, Kaiser, 102
WITSCH & SCHMITT, 20, 21

Zulu wars, 230

PICTURE CREDITS

Pictures of the following cigar boxes are copyright © 1997 Tony Hyman: *The Old Glory, The Smokers Pride, Champion, El Plantador, Defiance, Dew Drop, All Points, Cabin Home, Merry Christmas, Holiday Greetings, Compliments of the Season, Hustler, Recruit, Knaup's Diplomacy, Untitled (Pretty girl), Toboggans, Prize Winners, Winsome, Tom Moore, Pippins, 50/50, Apache Trail, War Eagle, Carême*. All other graphics in this book are copyright 1997 © Aaron Industries.